RICHARD WAGNER AND THE SYNTHESIS OF THE ARTS

RICHARD WAGNER

&

THE SYNTHESIS

OF THE ARTS

By Jack M. Stein

Department of Germanic Languages and Literature
Harvard University

GREENWOOD PRESS, PUBLISHERS
WESTPORT, CONNECTICUT

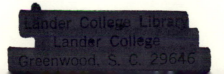

Library of Congress Cataloging in Publication Data

Stein, Jack Madison.
    Richard Wagner & the synthesis of the arts.

    Reprint of the ed. published by Wayne State
University Press, Detroit.
    Bibliography: p.
    1. Wagner, Richard, 1813-1883. 2. Music and
literature. I. Title.
[ML410.W1S83 1973]   782.1'092'4   73-1840
ISBN 0-8371-6806-6

Grateful acknowledgement is made to the Ford Foundation
for financial assistance in making possible the
publication of this volume.

Originally published in 1960 by Wayne State University
Press, Detroit

Reprinted with the permission of Wayne State University Press

First Greenwood Reprinting 1973
Second Greenwood Reprinting 1975

Library of Congress Catalog Card Number 73-1840

ISBN 0-8371-6806-6

Printed in the United States of America

To Isabel

Preface

THE APPARATUS of this work has been reduced to a minimum. There are few footnotes; references to other works have been made parenthetically in the text in a manner which, it is hoped, will be immediately clear to the reader upon consulting the bibliography. All works referred to in any way, even if there is no parenthetical reference, will likewise be found there.

All German quotations have been translated into English. With one exception, the translations are my own, although I have freely consulted others. Reference to the source of the translated quotations is to the original German in all but the one exception. The illustrations involving music have been taken from piano scores, since these are more readily accessible to the reader than are the full scores and since indication of the exact orchestration is not essential. It was necessary to retain the original German dialog in these examples, in order to show the poetic-musical synthesis. Literal translations have been added.

It is a pleasure to acknowledge my indebtedness to the many friends and colleagues who have assisted me, particularly to Professor Leo Schrade and Dr. John Firth. Most of all I am grateful for the wise counsel and generous advice of my former teacher, Professor T. M. Campbell. The opportunity to work for a full year in the *Staatsbibliothek* in Munich was made possible through the generosity of the Guggenheim Foundation and the Fulbright Commission. My thanks go also to the *Germanic Review* for permission to use portions of two articles of mine on Wagner which appeared in that journal.

J. M. S.

Table of Contents

RICHARD WAGNER AND THE SYNTHESIS OF THE ARTS

Introduction

A SYNTHESIS of the arts can take on many forms, from Greek tragedy to Gregorian chant, from South German Baroque interiors to the synesthesia of the Romantics. Since the Renaissance, the idea of synthesis has been associated most persistently with the stage, principally opera, which indeed originated in an attempt to revive the form of Greek tragedy. It was but a short time after the invention of opera that the intended synthesis of poetry, music, and stage action succumbed to the expressive power of music and became largely its vehicle. Yet the history of opera shows a number of attempts to restore a better balance among the components. The most celebrated of the reformers before Wagner was Gluck, whose preface to *Alceste* some hold to be as significant a document on the relationship between the arts of poetry and music as Wagner's voluminous theories. "When I undertook to set the opera *Alceste* to music," wrote Gluck, "it was my intention to avoid scrupulously all the abuses which the misplaced vanity of singers and the all-too-great tractability of composers have introduced into Italian opera. . . . I sought to bring music back to its true function, that is, to support the poetry and to strengthen the emotional expression and interest of the situations, without interrupting the action or distorting it by useless ornamentation." (M.G., 177) From this decision, modern opera, as distinguished from its Baroque predecessor, can be said to originate. Since Gluck's time most opera composers, among the Germans and Austrians before Wagner, principally Mozart, Beethoven, Marschner, and Weber, have considered the problem of musical declamation and the relation of text to music, but always from an interest heavily weighted toward music and without arriving at anything definitive or strikingly novel in the juxtaposition of the various elements.

The desire for a genuine synthesis has been more marked

among writers than among composers, and since Lessing and Herder there have been many German poets and literary theorists who have dealt with the problem. Lessing, as Max Koch points out, speculated on a synthesis which would respect the limitations of the separate arts while using them to supplement each other. This position has striking analogies to Wagner's *The Art-Work of the Future* and *Opera and Drama* (see p. 61). Herder was as convinced of the possibility of a union of the dramatic arts as he was scornful of the state of opera in his day. "There is no reason to doubt the exalted effect which an intelligent alliance of music, poetry, and the dance, these arts which so naturally belong together, would produce," he wrote. "The course of time will bring us a man who, scorning our present hodge-podge of wordless tones, will realize the necessity of an intimate union of purely human feeling and of the fable itself with the music. From the imperious elevation where the ordinary composer ostentatiously avers that poetry must serve his art, he will descend and . . . let his music serve the words of the emotion, of the action itself. . . . He will overturn the whole disorganized, ragged framework of operatic sing-song and erect . . . a cohesive lyric structure in which poetry, music, action, and decoration are all one." (H.W., XXIII, 336) Wagner partisans have cited this "prophecy" of Herder's ever since Karl Grunsky made it official by applying it to the master in an article in the sycophantic *Bayreuther Blätter*.

Alfred Neumann, in an unpublished dissertation, "The Evolution of the Concept of the *Gesamtkunstwerk* * in German Romanticism," tells of Wieland's efforts to improve the state of opera libretti. And of Goethe he writes, "With Philipp Christoph Kayser, Goethe wanted to write a through-composed Singspiel, a mixture between a *commedia dell' arte* and an *opera seria*. He spent long months in preparing the libretto, giving endless instructions to the composer and even aiding him with considerable funds in the hope of finding a new Gluck, only to fail because of the mediocre talent of the young composer." (Neumann, 76–77) Major portions of *Faust*, Part II, particularly the third act, are operatic, but the

---

* This term, which has no satisfactory English equivalent (total work of art?), has come to be associated principally with Wagner, although it was never used by him to mean art synthesis.

union of the arts envisioned by Goethe was never satisfactorily realized for the same reason that the attempted Singspiel failed. Schiller, too, experimented, without conspicuous success, with a *Gesamtkunstwerk* in his *Braut von Messina,* being of course unable to supply the music which he considered an indispensable part (see bibliography: Robert T. Clark, Jr.).

The Romantics longed for a synthesis of the arts, and Tieck, Wackenroder, Novalis, Brentano, Hoffmann, Runge and others either theorized about synthesis or experimented in it with mixed results (see bibliography: Othmar Fries, Alfred Neumann, Eugene Reed). Friedrich Schelling, chief philosopher of German Romanticism, who raised art to its dizziest pinnacle, seeing the universe itself as a perfect work of art (see bibliography: Kurt Knopf), ends his *Philosophy of Art* with the demand for a combination of all the arts that can possibly be brought onto the stage. (Neumann, 153–55) In general, these men were long on theory and short on practice, and in the Romantic period it was the composers who produced the most effective and powerful art synthesis. I refer to the development of the lied form by Schubert, Schumann, and others, a genuine and successful fusion of poetry and music into a larger unit, which, along with Beethoven's *Ninth,* must be considered the immediate forerunners of the syntheses of Richard Wagner.

It was Wagner who channeled the two major streams of experimentation, the musical-practical on the one hand, and the literary-theoretical on the other, into one. He was a composer of operas, of course; but (postponing any arguments as to the quality of his literary gifts) he was a poet and a theorist as well and drew freely from his predecessors in all fields to produce a large body of theory on synthesis, as well as a succession of practical counterparts of these theories. The purpose of the present work is to examine this central focus of Wagner's activity, the concept of a synthesis of the arts; to follow the germination and development of the idea in theory; and to analyze his works as experiments in art synthesis. In 1851, Wagner produced a major work of art theory, *Opera and Drama,* in which his early thinking, writing, and creating culminated. It was this theory which finally provided him with a firm basis for what he had been sporadically attempting in certain sections of his earlier works: the use of music as the most powerful means for emotional delineation of the psychology underlying the dramatic presentation. In the period of *Opera and Drama,* it was Wagner's conviction that this could best be done by subordinating the music to the total drama, making the latter the point of departure at all times, and working out with meticulous care the exact functions and practical interrelationships of the various contributing elements, including the music.

This has rightly been considered his central exposition of the *Gesamtkunstwerk.* It has not been generally recognized, however, that with his acceptance of Schopenhauer only three years after this theory, Wagner assumed a philosophic position which contradicted the very basis of *Opera and Drama.* This new circumstance affects the esthetics of every one of his works from *The Valkyrie* on, including *Siegfried, Twilight of the Gods, Tristan and Isolde, The Mastersingers,* and *Parsifal.* As a consequence, *Opera and Drama* becomes a very inadequate guide to Wagner's artistic impulse as it is expressed in these works, although writers on Wagner have continued to use it as the theoretical frame of reference from which to analyze them. Nietzsche was aware of the radical shift in esthetic belief and wrote in his *Genealogy of Morals,* "Let us consider the remarkable . . . position of Schopenhauer on art: for it is obviously this which caused Richard Wagner to go over to him . . . and this to the degree that a complete theoretical contradiction was opened up between his earlier and later esthetic beliefs—the former as expressed in *Opera and Drama,* for example, the latter in the writings published from 1870 on" (Nietzsche, III, 5), but to this day the consequences of this major change have not been drawn.

Schopenhauer ruled out the possibility of a synthesis, and it was Wagner's problem in the ensuing years to bring about a reconciliation between Schopenhauer's theories of music and his own artistic need for a union of the arts. This interesting process can be followed in his theory and practice from 1854 on. In his theory, there are three major stages: "Music of the Future," an essay in which a tentative attempt is made to realign the elements of the *Gesamtkunstwerk* of the *Opera and Drama* in accord with Schopenhauer's doctrines; *Beethoven,* in which an entirely new theory of synthesis is worked out, using Schopenhauer's theories as a point of departure; and *The Destiny of Opera,* where a new and interesting variation of the *Beethoven* theory is evolved. The works parallel this development, with *Tristan and Isolde* closest to "Music of the Future"; *The Mastersingers* to *The Destiny of Opera;* and *Parsifal* to *Beethoven.* An analysis of these and the other works from the point of view of Wagner's beliefs at the time of their composition will necessarily differ from the view that has hitherto been taken of them.

It will be seen in the course of my examination that *Opera and Drama* is a curious combination of Romantic ideas, the esthetic rationalism of Lessing, and the materialistic sensationalism of Ludwig Feuerbach. At a later stage, Wagner attempts to superimpose upon this already heterogeneous structure Schopenhauer's metaphysics of music, and still later abandons his original ideas on the limitations of the various arts, and his Feuerbachian materialism, to swing over entirely to a metaphysical view of art and art synthesis. All this sounds, and is, eclectic in the bad sense, and would be an automatic condemnation of Wagner as a theorist if we were inclined to consider him an original philosopher. This is not the case, however. Wagner had no original philosophic ideas which can be respected as such. The importance of his theories rests not in themselves, but rather in the light they throw on his artistic activities. But in spite of his extensive theorizing, Wagner was primarily an intuitive artist. His theory is more often conditioned by his practice than the other way around, and it is necessary to deal with it chiefly because an accurate picture of the creative process in Wagner can be obtained only by considering theory and practice as reciprocal and complementary aspects of his creativity.

As a *Gesamtkünstler,* Wagner felt impelled to operate in numerous fields at once, both in theory and in practice. He is consequently vulnerable to the imputation made by Thomas Mann in his "Suffering and Greatness of Richard Wagner" that he was a dilettante through and through, in the sense that he was nowhere thoroughly at home and authoritative, even in music, and, being impelled to take all art as his province, had to operate in a variety of fields at once, in none of which he was a specialist.

Mann cautions that his remarks must not be understood as un-
equivocally derogatory and further characterizes Wagner's art as
"dilettantism, monumentalized and elevated to the realm of genius
by his extreme will power and intelligence." (Mann, 413)

Wagner himself virtually admits his "dilettantism" in a letter
to Johannes Nordmann, reported by Guido Adler in his book on
Wagner. "It probably surprises you that I do not go to someone
else for my texts, but prepare my own. Aside from the fact that
you craftsmen can never correctly feel the musical rhythm which
we need, your verses are much too pedantic, strict and scholastic
for us. You have, as your Nestroy so rightly says in his *Lumpazi-
vagabundus*, 'learned your astronomy from the book.' For me tone
and word must spring spontaneously and simultaneously from
heart and head and the one must join the other as in a passionate
kiss. Now, I can scarcely see how anyone can require someone
else's intervention and assistance at such an act of love. This is why
I take care of the matter without a companion. What I create in
the future in this regard will perhaps present me in a light which
might be considered too glaring for the trained poet. But I should
not be reproached for going my own way, and in the very near
future I will be striking out in a direction which lies far afield
from the main road." (Adler, 58–59)

The interrelationship between the various facets of his artistic
nature is well illustrated by the successive stages in the creation
of his works. After extensive research, and various preliminary
sketches in prose and verse, he would write the complete text before beginning with the composition. (The very few instances
where he had a previous musical inspiration, as for example the
prize song from *The Mastersingers,* are exceptions and cannot
fairly be cited as proof of the opposite in view of his otherwise
unvarying practice.) But, as he himself states (W.S., IV, 316–17),
the intended musical setting of the words he was writing conditioned at all times in an indefinable way the configuration of the
poetic line. Once the text was finished and composition begun,
the words of course exerted a decisive influence on the musical
configuration; yet here too there was no single direction of influence. The original texts were invariably altered in hundreds of
minor but often significant ways to adjust them to the musical pat-

terns as they developed. In a letter to Liszt of December 6, 1856, Wagner writes, "One of these days I will be finished with the first scene [of *Siegfried*]. Strange, only in writing the music for them does the essential meaning of my poems dawn on me; everywhere I discover secrets which until then had remained well hidden even from me." (W.L., II, 143)

It is possible that Wagner's vulnerability in the partial is but the reverse of his strength in the total; at any rate, it is in the validity of the total effort, art synthesis, that Wagner's artistic contribution should be evaluated. The present work proposes to do this in three ways which, in spite of the vast body of Wagnerian research, have not yet been tried. It will keep the whole view; the *Gesamtkunstwerk* idea will be the only frame of reference, and the separate phases of art, in Wagner's theory and practice, will be considered only in their relation to the idea of a synthesis. It will examine in close detail both theory and works; no study exists which has extracted the exact picture of the *Gesamtkunstwerk* from the total body of the far-ranging Wagnerian theory, and consequently no detailed correlation between theory and practice in this regard has been possible. And finally, it will for the first time discuss the theories on synthesis developed by Wagner subsequent to his major essay, *Opera and Drama,* and relate the works after 1854 to his changing views. It is hoped that the result will be a new and more accurate picture of Richard Wagner as both theorist and creative artist.

chapter one
Before Rienzi

IF WAGNER had died as young as Büchner or Keats, we would have had no inkling of his greatness. His first published work, *Rienzi,* was finished in 1840 when he was twenty-seven years old, and even it is far from being a masterpiece. Before this he had written a considerable quantity of music, including a symphony and two full-length operas, and some literary works, including at least one drama. We do not possess any of the earlier literary efforts, but it seems safe to take Wagner's word for their juvenile character. Much of the early music is extant; it is all highly derivative and imitative; none of it, with the possible exception of parts of the two operas, worth the effort of rehearsal and performance time. *The Fairies* (1834) is second-rate Weber and Marschner and *The Ban on Love* (1836) is second- or third-rate Auber and Bellini.

The drastic switch in models between the two operas is itself a good indication that Wagner had not yet found his true voice. Auber and Bellini represented the main stream of Italian and French opera tradition, which, certain differences notwithstanding, together dominated the European operatic world. Their works were "grand" operas, suitable for spectacular presentation at the Paris opera and they culminated in Wagner's day in the great triumphs of Meyerbeer. The German opera tradition, represented by Marschner and Weber, was a quite different matter. Derived from the eighteenth-century Singspiel rather than from the grand opera tradition of the Baroque era, they were on a smaller scale, demanded far less by way of show and spectacle, and were in general more like musical dramas than operatic pageants.

Wagner's shift in allegiance from native German works to French and Italian opera was the result of his contact with the usual repertory in his various posts as conductor, in Würzburg, Lauchstädt, Rudolstadt, Magdeburg, Königsberg, and Riga, from 1833 on until he went to Paris in 1839. As Ernest Newman puts it, "his superficial theatrical experience had given him something of a distaste for the heavier German music, and so made him peculiarly susceptible to the expert eclecticism of Meyerbeer." (E.N., I, 225– 26) Wagner seems to have been a natural born operatic conductor and apparently was able to make Meyerbeer *et al.* sound better than they really were.

At any rate, his essays of this period, his first theoretical writing, are full of praise for French and Italian opera and of scorn for the German tradition. He is contemptuous of German attempts to "intellectualize" opera. On the first page of his first essay, "German Opera," he makes the claim that the Germans are too intellectual and learned to create warm human figures. Of Weber's *Euryanthe* he writes: "What petty pedantry in the declamation—what fussy use of one instrument or another in support of the expression of every single word!" (W.S., XII, 2) The whole fabric of the opera, he says, is riddled by so much attention to petty details. Wagner criticized all attempts to support the dramatic element by comments of the various instruments or harmonic nuances intended to make clear the dramatic design. He spoke of the "eternally allegorizing orchestral tumult," deriding in general all those aspects of dramatic music which appeared in Weber's works (and which Wagner was later to develop to their ultimate complexity).

Song, pure unencumbered melodic utterance, in other words, the aria of the French and Italian school, was his current enthusiasm. Song, he declared, is the only language in which a human being can communicate musically, and it must remain as free and independent as any other type of language if it is to be understood. Such expressions as "noble song" and "clear melodious thought" appeared continually throughout his early essays. "Song, song, and again I say, song," he wrote in "Bellini." (W.S., XII, 20) To the orchestra he devoted no attention at all.

In a letter to Meyerbeer from Riga in 1837, he goes so far as to regret his early enthusiasm for Beethoven. This, he claimed, had adversely affected his early attempts at opera. He had been set straight by his contact with the standard operatic repertory and particularly with the works of Meyerbeer. Only by taking the Italian and French schools as models could the German opera composer hope to create masterpieces. One might be tempted to discount this as mere flattery of the famous man (Wagner was not above currying favor) if it did not coincide exactly with what we find elsewhere. In "Bellini" he wrote: "When we consider the limitless disorder, the jumble of forms, periods, and modulations of so many modern German composers, which so often rob us of the enjoyment of frequent individual beauties, we often wish this disorder could be regulated by the stable form of Italian opera. As a matter of fact, the instantaneous clear comprehension of a passion on the stage is made vastly more easy when that passion, along with all its allied feelings and emotions, is expressed in one bold stroke by a single clear comprehensible melody than when it is undermined and in the long run intellectualized away by a hundred petty commentaries, by this or that harmonic nuance, by the interjection of one instrument or another." (W.S., XII, 20) All this is of course the reverse of what Wagner stands for today in the development of opera. One could scarcely devise a position more exactly in contradiction to his later attitude. It is another proof of his slow start. Years later, in a letter to Mathilde Wesendonck (June 9, 1862) he claims to remember having been in serious doubt when he was about thirty whether he had the stuff in him for independent productivity. "I could still detect influence and imitation in my works and looked with grave misgivings toward my future development as a creative artist." (M.W., 305)

A careful reading of the early essays yields only one spot where the voice of the later Wagner makes itself heard. In a pseudonymous article, "Pasticcio," written for Schumann's *Neue Zeitschrift für Musik* in 1834, Wagner says that the essence of dramatic art is to portray the inner nature of human life and action. This the French and Italian operas of his time fail to do. They are predominantly a series of musical numbers without psychological connection. In order to bring the drama and the music into better balance, he continues, the masterly declamation and effective dramatic art of Gluck must be blended with the contrasting melodic lines of Mozart. The statement is significant in so far as it is the first indication of Wagner's recognition of the problem of the dramatic authenticity of opera, but it is an isolated remark, not developed until a later period.

chapter two
Rienzi

RIENZI is Wagner's first published work and the first opera of his to be given a successful performance. It is also the last and most grandiose of the derivative works which he seemed to need to get out of his system before settling down once and for all to writing Wagnerian works properly so called. Ernest Newman calls it a "bad attack of musical measles" (W.M.A., 261), and indeed few writers have much to say in its favor. Even Wagner made few claims for it later. In 1860 he wrote: "Let me briefly mention an opera which preceded *The Flying Dutchman: Rienzi.* . . . To this work, which owed its conception and formal execution to my earliest impressions of Spontini's heroic operas as well as the brilliant genre of Parisian grand opera by Auber, Meyerbeer, and Halévy, I attach no special importance, because it contains no single essential feature of the artistic concepts which later manifested themselves in my works." (W.S., VII, 119)

Yet it is an interesting starting point for my analysis because it has much in common with the early essays I have been discussing, while at the same time certain tentative signs of the Wagner to come show through the seams, if one's eyes are sharp enough. Paul Bekker, in *Richard Wagner, His Life in His Work,* has argued that *Rienzi* falls into two distinct styles, the division occurring between Acts II and III. To him the first two acts are heroic grand opera in the Italian and French style, while Acts III to V show considerable evidence of transition in the direction of *The Flying Dutchman.*

The chronology of composition would support such a distinction. The poem was written in its entirety in the summer of 1838. The first two acts were composed, except for the scoring, immediately afterward, between the summer of 1838 and May, 1839, at

Riga. It was not until nine months later, during which Wagner took up residence in Paris, that Act III was commenced. Acts III, IV, and V were composed from February 15 to September 19, 1840, in Paris, and in the following year, *The Flying Dutchman* was begun and finished. The time element is of great importance, for it is during the early part of Wagner's stay in Paris that he experienced a change of heart about the glories of heroic grand opera and began to sound like a quite different person in his essays. The first two acts of *Rienzi* reflect the admiration of traditional opera that his youthful essays revealed. The later acts show the transition from this attitude to the opinions of the Paris essays and novellas, particularly *A Pilgrimage to Beethoven,* which we will discuss in the next chapter.

The text of *Rienzi* is in conventional iambic verse, usually with four accents to the line, often rhymed and frequently changing to blank verse during Rienzi's speeches. It is of no special interest to us, since it contains none of the elements Wagner later began to introduce into his poetry in order to bring word and tone into a more intimate relation. We may accept without hesitation his own later characterization of it as a "good, not trivial opera libretto." (W.S., IV, 259) The transition from the conventional operatic technique to the more characteristically Wagnerian style is to be sought for in the music.

In the first two acts, the customary alternation between recitative and aria is the rule. In the former there is almost no musical interest, the melodic line simply adjusting itself unobtrusively to the declamatory accents of the verse:

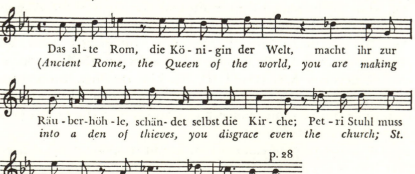

Das al-te Rom, die Kö-ni-gin der Welt,   macht ihr zur
(Ancient Rome, the Queen of the world, you are making

Räu-ber-höh-le, schän-det selbst die Kir-che; Pet-ri Stuhl muss
into a den of thieves, you disgrace even the church; St.

p. 28

flüch-ten zum fer-nen A-vig-non;
Peter's throne must flee to distant Avignon;)

This is a thoroughly typical example of traditional recitative and scarcely needs any comment. Nevertheless, in order to establish certain practical esthetic principles which will become increasingly important in the course of the discussion, a partial analysis follows. A series of brief practical expositions at all stages will, I trust, be more acceptable than the exhaustive analyses which would otherwise become necessary with the later more complex relationships. The relationship of word and tone in the musical dialog is the central feature of Wagner's *Gesamtkunstwerk* and a detailed chronological analysis of this relationship is one of the chief aims of this book.

The musical line in the above example supplements in an entirely banal way the normal accent of the verse form. The accents of the verse ("R*o*m," "Königin," "W*e*lt," "R*äu*berhöhle," etc.) fall consistently on the strongest beats of the measure, either the first or third. The unaccented syllables are distributed among the various unaccented portions of the measure so that they receive no undue stress. In actual performance even more exact differentiation between important and unimportant syllables can be achieved, since there is nothing to prevent a slight differentiation in length between two notes or more which are of equal value in the printed score (as in "Königin der"). The accompaniment consists only of short chords. The accented syllables are consistently placed on relatively important scale pitch ("Rom" on the mediant, "Welt," because it contains a slight intensification, on the more important dominant, etc.) and further accentuation is accomplished by use of higher pitches for more important moments, especially when a large skip is involved (as in "schändet").

The musical line in recitative of this kind is governed solely by the demands of the poetic line. It is little more than an operatic convention to avoid the use of spoken dialog. Yet it is essentially this part of traditional opera rather than its esthetically more significant features, the arias, choruses, and ensembles, that Wagner gradually transforms into the musical dialog of his greatest works.

In the aria, the situation is reversed. It progresses in accordance with the structural needs of the melody, and only a most nominal attention is paid to fitting the musical to the poetic phrase. Where there is any clash, and there usually is, the musical phrase is the determining factor. This causes frequent distortion of verse accent and rhythm:

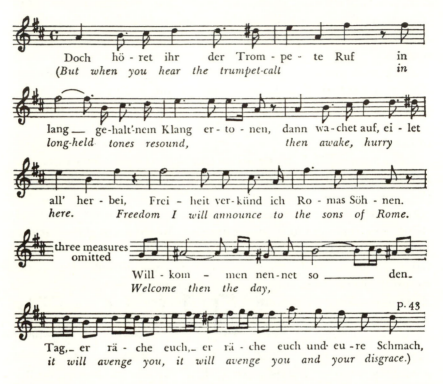

Doch   hö - ret   ihr   der   Trom - pe - te   Ruf   in
(*But   when   you   hear   the   trumpet-call*   *in*

lang __ ge-halt'-nem Klang er - to - nen, dann wa-chet auf, ei - let
long-held   tones   resound,   then   awake,   hurry

all' her - bei, Frei - heit ver-künd ich Ro - mas Söh - nen.
here.   Freedom   I   will   announce   to   the   sons   of   Rome.

three measures omitted

Will - kom - men nen-net so _____ den.
Welcome   then   the   day,

P· 43

Tag,__ er   rä - che   euch,__ er   rä - che   euch und· eu -re   Schmach,
it   will   avenge   you,   it   will   avenge   you   and   your   disgrace.)

It is quite clear in this example that a melody was composed which coincides rhythmically in only the most general way with the rhythm of the verse, and which is worked out according to a purely melodic pattern without further reference to the words. Note how the exigencies of the melodic line cause syllables which should be stressed to fall into unaccented positions ("höret," "wachet," "eilet"), and vice versa ("doch," "ihr," "dann," "Frei*heit*"). The correct delivery of the melodic line requires, of course, a steady tempo, which adds a further note of distortion to the rhythm of the lines. The musical phrase progresses up or down, from less to more emphatic notes of the scale and from higher to lower pitch, according to its own pattern and without regard to the sense or rhythm of the verse. The lengthening of the vowels is also purely musical, and not related to the words. The appropriateness of the two-and-three-quarter beats on the word "lang" is quite accidental, as a glance at the other held notes, particularly in the second section of the example, will show. As the musical pattern is worked out, less and less attention is given to the verse (from "Willkommen" on).

Moments of more intensely dramatic interest are by no means lacking in the first two acts of *Rienzi*. These take the form of a more elaborately conceived free declamation with a fuller orchestra accompaniment. It is in these sections, if anywhere in the first two acts, that the future Wagner is in evidence, although the technique, a kind of heightened recitative, is commonly found in operas of the period. One of the best musical-dramatic scenes in this section of the work occurs at the point where Colonna reveals to his son, Adriano, the existence of a plot to assassinate Rienzi:

The musical rhythm is carefully subordinated to the poetic declamation; the dramatic pauses are especially effective. At the same time, the melodic line intensifies the ominous effect of the verse by the insistent repetition on one note, in contrast to the usual flexibility of pitch. As the climax of the poetic phrase is approached, there is a sudden rise to E♭ on a note sustained for a full measure. After another dramatic pause, there occurs an additional half step rise in pitch (to E on "weisst's," involving a sudden modulation), followed by a swift descent on the word "Verworf'ner."

The orchestra is noisily present throughout all of *Rienzi,* but no special significance attaches to it in the first two acts with reference to the later developments in orchestra delineation which are to play such an important role in the *Gesamtkunstwerk.* It is used only for harmonic support of the most conventional nature, a fact which is consistent with Wagner's disregard of the orchestra in his prose writing of this time.

Wagner's use of the technique of the recurrent musical phrase, or leitmotif, in the first two acts of *Rienzi* is, with one exception, not particularly noteworthy. There are several orchestral motifs which recur later but which do not carry this technique beyond the preliminary state in which it is to be found frequently in pre-Wagnerian opera, from Monteverdi to Weber. There is one motif which can be considered a forerunner of the "motif of reminiscence," the kind of leitmotif which will later have the most powerful unifying effect on the *Gesamtkunstwerk.* The nature and use of these is most fully explained in *Opera and Drama,* Wagner's major essay on the synthesis of the arts (see pp. 74 ff.). They are motifs which are drawn from a specific poetic-melodic line and are thereafter always associated with the original words. They occur only very rarely in the works before *Opera and Drama.* The motif in question here is the Vengeance motif, first sung by Rienzi in Act I as a threat of vengeance on the nobles who have killed his younger brother:

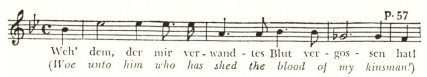

p. 57

Weh' dem, der mir ver - wand - tes Blut ver - gos - sen hat!
(*Woe unto him who has shed the blood of my kinsman!*)

The same musical line, slightly altered, appears twice more in the first two acts, each time connected with the idea of vengeance. Once it is repeated by Rienzi, as an inner sense warns him of the consequences attendant on his carrying out the threat, to the words, "Was willst du, düstre Ahnung, mir?" ("What do you want of me, gloomy foreboding?"). (*Rienzi,* 143) Farther on, it is sung by Adriano, as a threat of vengeance on Rienzi if the latter should carry out the death sentence on Adriano's father, to the words, "Gib mir verwandtes Blut zu rächen" ("Give me the blood of a relative to avenge"). (*Rienzi,* 147)

With the beginning of Act III, the sharp division between recitative and aria disappears. Bare recitative occurs only infrequently, for the most part giving way to a more dramatic kind of declamation which attempts to exploit the emotional possibilities inherent in the melodic line for the purpose of underlining the dramatic effect of the words. The orchestral accompaniment of this dramatic recitative becomes continuous and adds some harmonic weight of its own to the emotional interpretation of the phrase. The following is a typical example:

It can be seen at once that this kind of dialog resembles that in Wagner's mature works considerably more than does the quotation on page 16. However, no extravagant claims can be made for this, since musical dialog similar to the above can also be found in the works of Spontini and others. The difference between this musical-poetic line and the recitative of *Rienzi* quoted earlier rests in the increased esthetic importance of the musical line. The melodic contour is assimilated to the natural declamatory accents and rhythms of the verse, as in the earlier type of recitative, but the music is no longer negligible. By its own inherent dramatic beauty, it contributes to the total effect of the musical-poetic line. Since it is fitted to the characteristics of the verse and does not shape a formal pattern of its own, as in the example from the aria form, page 18, it does not draw the attention away from the poetic line by its intrinsic beauty. Rather, it fixes the interest more securely upon the verse by heightening the contrasts, highlighting the accents, and expanding the sensuous content of the accented vowel sounds.

This quotation well illustrates some of the chief problems Wagner was going to have to overcome in the construction of the word-tone synthesis in his later works. The increased importance of the musical line draws him into some unnatural declamations: "und," in the third measure, receives an undue stress; similarly "war," in the tenth bar. The entire phrase, "Ich halt' ihn jetzt" is not well assimilated by the musical line. As Wagner gradually becomes more expert, such awkward spots become less and less frequent. Furthermore, the attempt to fit the music to the natural declamatory rhythm of the verse, and at the same time to give the musical aspect added importance, results in musical banalities which have sacrificed the melodic beauty of the formal aria without actually attaining any dramatic emotional significance in its place; in the above example, "um jedes Band" to "Ich halt' ihn jetzt" is very weak musically and dramatically.

However, there are also unmistakable signs of the later Wagner, particularly in the first five and the last five measures. The half-measure pause after the word "schwur" brings what follows into greater relief and also permits both the strongly accented "schwur" and the equally strong "Tod" each to fall on the downbeat of its respective measure. "Verderben" receives a similar downbeat accent in the next bar and is brought further into relief by the rise in pitch and the change in harmony. In this way, both musically and poetically, there is an increase in intensity, reaching its peak on "Verderben." The downward course of the entire fourth measure, plus the strikingly accurate rhythmic assimilation of the triplet on "solle mir," increases the emotional and dramatic effect. The "Losung," which poetically requires an accent, but not as strong a one as those which precede it, is placed at the lowest point of the descending line, thus reducing to just the right proportion the accentual effect of its position on the downbeat of the measure.

In the last five measures, the functional expansion of the sensuous content of the accented vowels is a striking means of increasing the musical-poetic effect. This extension of the vowels, which underlines the emotional content inherent in the individual word itself, is perhaps the most noteworthy improvement in the declamatory technique of this part of *Rienzi*, although here again no extravagant claims can be made. This is a time-honored technique, used instinctively by many composers. It is of special interest to us here only because Wagner later makes a conscious esthetic principle of it and develops its expressive effectiveness to an unprecedented degree. In the above example, the four beats on "Tod" naturally focus attention on the word. The fact that the held note progresses from the third beat of the bar through the normally strongest beat of the succeeding measure creates a psychological intensification which further increases the emotional content of the word itself. The climax of the entire phrase is reached by the measure-long vowel extension on "Verderben," as well as the rise to a brilliant A♭, followed by an expressive pause for two beats, which sets it off.

This kind of musical-poetic line represents the initial stage in the transformation of formal recitative into the musical dialog of Wagner's later works. With each succeeding work we will see his hand growing surer, until the technique reaches its most perfect form in the *Ring* dramas and *Tristan and Isolde*. The progress to be noted in the three operas immediately to follow (i.e., *The Flying Dutchman, Tannhäuser,* and *Lohengrin*) will not involve any alteration in poetic technique. It is not until after *Lohengrin* that Wagner felt the need for a radical alteration of the verse form in order to attain a fuller word-tone synthesis.

Generally speaking, the tyranny of rigid alternation between recitative and aria is broken in the later acts of *Rienzi*. Frequently the arias do not have the formal musical structure and the sharp distinction from recitative that exist in the earlier acts. It is sometimes difficult to determine whether a particular passage is part of an aria or is the new type of recitative.

That is not to say that the traditional set aria has been entirely replaced. It does occur, as in Rienzi's prayer, in Act V, where the verse is subordinated to a clearly defined melodic pattern, which considerably distorts the rhythm of the verse:

Mein_____ Herr und Va - ter, O blik - ke her - ab,
(My Lord and Father, oh, look down,

sen - - ke dein Au - ge aus dei - nen___ Höh'n!
look down from your heights!)

P. 340

The orchestra in the later acts takes on considerably more importance. The texture is richer and the accompaniment is fuller and more continuous. The orchestra begins to stand out as a more independent body. The most significant advance in the orchestral fabric is the increased complexity of the leitmotif. Changes in harmonic coloring of the leitmotif occur to conform to changes in the mood of the scene. Perhaps the most striking example is the Santo Spirito Cavaliere motif sung by the chorus in the finale to Act III, which later comes to be identified with Rienzi himself and is powerfully sounded in rich minor chords at the moment of his final downfall.

The chorus in *Rienzi* plays a very important role, but only in the traditional operatic sense. Wagner's treatment of the chorus does not become interestingly novel until *Lohengrin*. It is possibly the element which gave him most trouble in his experiments with a synthesis of the arts and will be discussed at length at the proper time. In *Rienzi* and the following works, however, there is nothing of importance to be said about the chorus in this regard.

Rienzi in its total effect is predominantly "grand opera." The appearance of new elements in the latter half must not be over-emphasized. During an actual performance, the new features, although readily apparent to the discerning listener, would for the most part be submerged by the weight of the elements which are still in the grand opera tradition. Yet, as Paul Bekker makes clear, the differences in the two halves of *Rienzi* are all differences which point to *The Flying Dutchman* and beyond to Wagner's later development. Although even the latter part of *Rienzi* is a far cry from *The Ring of the Nibelung*, it undeniably does show the first faint traces of the later Wagner.

chapter three

Prose of the Paris and Dresden Periods

THE DREARY months of Wagner's stay in Paris (1839–42) were most significant for his development. They caused him to take a closer look at his models and to think more carefully about the bases of his art. What he saw in Paris convinced him that the French and Italian styles represented the past and not the future. He turned away from them forever. I do not mean to imply that this change of heart was exclusively a matter of esthetics. Contributing factors were the sheer impossibility of his piercing the magic circle surrounding the Paris opera, the misery and hunger forced upon him by his inability to get *Rienzi* performed, and a radical political attitude which saw in the Paris opera tradition the very fortress of conservatism and aristocracy.

On the other hand, it was not only politics and disappointed ambition which caused the change. Wagner was maturing artistically. *The Flying Dutchman* followed hard on the heels of *Rienzi,* and this was a work which unmistakably heralded the later Wagner. It very clearly implied a break with Paris and because of its advanced style was even destined to get a luke-warm reception on the German stage.

The various essays, novellas, and reports of the period show that Wagner was beginning to grapple with the problems of his art, after having for so long ridden along on the surface of them. He was also beginning to develop a prose style, although it was not yet free of imitation. Some of his reports of musical conditions in Paris are a weak imitation of Heine. The novellas of the Paris period are an even feebler imitation of E. T. A. Hoffmann's musical stories, and they owe a heavy debt to some of that writer's ideas on the function of music. Worst of all, they are shot through with the gross chauvinism toward the French that was to remain an unfortunate blemish on a great deal of Wagner's prose from then on.

Yet they contain some interesting discourses and some challenging ideas. In them Wagner delves into the problem of the nature of music for the first time. In "A Happy Evening," a dialog very reminiscent of Hoffmann's "The Poet and the Composer," Wagner writes that the language of music is eternal, infinite, ideal. It expresses nothing specific; not the passion, the love, the longing of this or that individual, but passion, love, longing themselves, in the abstract, and in the most universal terms. This is the peculiar characteristic of music alone, as distinguished from any other art. Program music he rejects categorically. The sphere of music is the indefinite, and it is impossible to convey any concrete impression through it. The same piece of music says not one thing to all, but many different things to different people at different times, and it is ridiculous for the composer or the commentator to attempt to force a specific pattern upon the listener. (W.S., 1, 143) Wagner's discussion is as much concerned with defining the limitations of music as with its potentialities. It argues the mutual exclusiveness of the arts and rejects the romantic idea of musical poetry and poetic music in the clearest terms. It is the position Wagner was to maintain later in great detail in his *Opera and Drama*.

Yet, clearly as he denies the validity of a "program" for a given piece of music, he is guilty of having constructed one in his explanatory program to Beethoven's *Ninth Symphony,* written for a performance under his direction in Dresden in 1846. Here he chooses quotations from *Faust* to elucidate this enigmatical work. For all his protestations that his quotations are not meant as a "program" but are rather atmospheric suggestions about the general nature and mood of the various parts of the symphony, it is a "program" nonetheless and stands in contradiction to what he has maintained elsewhere in this period.

Although he has commenced to define music clearly in the terms which he will later use in his outline for the *Gesamtkunst-werk* in *Opera and Drama,* he has not yet found a way to integrate it with the drama. In this matter there is a good deal of confusion in what he writes during this period. "It cannot be denied," he contends in an essay on the overture, "that the independence of purely musical production must suffer by being subordinated to a dramatic idea . . . and the composer, if he insists on depicting the details of the action, can not carry out his dramatic theme without causing his musical work to crumble to pieces." (W.S., I, 198)

Yet in the same essay, he adumbrates a technique foreshadowing his later use of leitmotif, whose very function is musical delineation of the action. "The composer [should] weave into the characteristic themes of his overture certain melodic or rhythmic features which later assume importance in the dramatic action. This importance would rest upon the fact that such passages are not strewn at random into the dramatic action but enter decisively and so to speak as landmarks for orientation into a specific aspect of human action. In this way they provide individuality to the overture as well." (W.S., I, 204)

The relationship of music and words, the central feature of his *Gesamtkunstwerk* of *Opera and Drama*, is still very much up in the air. "It is a misfortune," he writes, "that so many people have devoted themselves to the useless task of mixing the languages of music and poetry with one another and to try to complete or replace by the one what is in their opinion incomplete in the other." (W.S., I, 140)

In the best of Wagner's Hoffmannesque novellas, *A Pilgrimage to Beethoven* (1840), he sketches a plan for the ideal operatic form which foreshadows his later theories more clearly than any other statement before *Opera and Drama*. Beethoven is speaking of his troubles with *Fidelio* and vows he will never again write for the operatic stage. "If I were to write an opera to my liking the people would run away; for it would contain no arias, duets, trios, and all the other stuff with which an opera is patched together these days. Yet what I would replace it with no singer would sing and no audience would listen to." Beethoven would combine the orchestra and the human voice in a kind of *Gesamtkunstwerk*. The instruments of the orchestra, he says, represent the primal organs of nature, capable of expressing only elemental emotions, vague but powerful, while the human voice represents the human heart and its more individualized emotion. The capabilities of the orchestra for expression are manifold but indefinite. Those of the voice are limited but definite and precise. In an intimate combination of these two would lie an immense emotional appeal which would run the gamut from the most universal to the most individual.

Yet, according to Wagner's Beethoven, even in this plan the problem of how to unite words and music remains unsolved. Who could create poetry which would be worthy to stand with such expressiveness? "Poetry must be found wanting in such a combination, for words are too weak a vehicle for this task." (W.S., I, 111) In the final movement of my new symphony, Beethoven tells his visitor, you will see how I have tried to combine the human voice and the orchestra, but even the words of Schiller were too frail a vehicle to match the power of vocal and orchestral music combined.

Six years later, Wagner sees a solution to the word-tone problem in this final movement of Beethoven's *Ninth*. In his aforementioned explanatory program, he senses in the introduction to the last movement music different in nature from anything that had preceded it. Wagner reasoned that Beethoven was here struggling to express something more definite than music alone can express. Being instinctively aware of the limitations of music, he brought the music in the introductory section to the point where it most nearly approached the descriptive power of poetic verse and at that point actually did introduce poetry. The latter, thus prepared for, seemed a fulfillment of the drive toward concrete expression revealed by the altered character of the music. "With the beginning of the final movement Beethoven's music takes on a decidedly more articulate character: it departs from the sphere of purely instrumental music held to in the first three movements, where the expression is infinite and indefinite. The progress of the musical composition presses toward a climactic decision, a decisiveness which can be expressed only by the human voice. We are awed by the manner in which the master prepares for the entrance of speech and the human voice as an expected necessity by the deeply stirring recitative for bass instruments, which, itself almost departing from the boundaries of absolute music, confronts the other instruments, pressing for a decision, as though with powerful, emotionally moving speech." (W.S., II, 60)

One would almost feel tempted to find here the crucial example which revealed to Wagner all the possibilities of poetic-melodic union which he went on to develop in *Opera and Drama*, were it not for the fact that already three years earlier he had completed *Tannhäuser,* which contains verse and music much more intimately blended than in Beethoven's *Ninth Symphony*. There seems little doubt, however, that his interpretation of the choral movement from Beethoven's symphony played a decisive role in bridging the gap between the intuitive and the conscious solution of the word-tone problem.

chapter four

The Flying Dutchman

IN GENERAL, Wagner's progress toward an art synthesis can be observed more concretely in the succession of works, *The Flying Dutchman* (1841), *Tannhäuser* (1845), and *Lohengrin* (1848), than in the uncertain and sporadic theorizing he did about it in this decade. This was a period of largely intuitive experimentation. Although *The Flying Dutchman* is still recognizably in the operatic tradition, there is no mistaking the future Wagner in many of its pages. In a way, it is a very curious mixture of the old and the new. Much of it is in the style of the formal operatic number: the aria, duet, trio, etc. It contains a number of Italianate tunes that have a lilt and pleasant charm, for all the world like Bellini or Auber or Meyerbeer. Schumann recognized this, and said so in a letter to Wagner after an examination of the score at Wagner's invitation. Having repudiated Meyerbeer completely by this time, Wagner found Schumann's comments most unwelcome. We can believe that it took some restraint for him to have replied, "I agree with you in all that you say about my operas, as far as your present state of knowledge of them goes. Only one thing took me aback, and—I must admit—caused me some bitterness; that you could so calmly say that much had a Meyerbeerian flavor. First of all, I have no idea what in the world could be called Meyerbeerian, except perhaps a sly striving for shallow popularity. It is impossible for anything definite to be Meyerbeerian, for in this sense Meyerbeer himself is not Meyerbeerian, but rather Rossinian, Bellinian, Auberian, Spontinian and so on and so on. If there really were something consistent which could be called Meyerbeerian, such as one can call certain things Beethovenesque, or for that matter Rossinian, I confess that it would be a miracle if I had drawn from *that* spring whose very odor is repulsive to me from afar. Such a thing would be the death sentence for my productive capacity." (R.W.F., 28–29)

But the Dionysian Wagner is also present in *The Flying Dutchman*. The demands of the dramatic situation begin to transform the musical expression into a vehicle for the fuller exploitation of the emotional intensity of the drama, rather than to give occasion for musical expression which more or less uses the dramatic scene as a springboard. Particularly at the moments of highest psychological tension, a rich emotional impact is attained by a kind of impassioned music which leaves the Apollonian shores of his pretty tunes far behind. One is never sure when this new kind of overwhelmingly and intensely emotional writing will appear, and the mood shifts back and forth from intensity to relative placidity in a somewhat bewildering way. Thus it is easy for the listener who came to hear the more intense Wagner to become impatient with the continual interruption by the set pieces, while the listener who wants to enjoy the opera in *The Flying Dutchman* can easily resent the emotionality and expressiveness of the other passages.

The importance of this change in the character of the relationship between the music and the dramatic situation is basic. It is Wagner's most significant contribution to the development of the lyric drama, and it opens up an entirely new facet in the opera form. It is the reason why Wagner was able later to claim that all his predecessors in the development of opera, even such innovators as Monteverdi and Gluck, failed to alter the basic ingredients of the operatic form. For, although Gluck, for example, placed great importance on declamation and on the assimilation of the mood of the text to the spirit of the music, the latter in Gluck never ceases to be the central consideration and the dramatic situation is never elevated to the importance it attains sometimes in *The Flying Dutchman* and gradually more consistently thereafter. The drive to imbue music with dramatic intensity to the disregard of formal musical elements was never before present in the degree it exists in Wagner.

And there is no end to it; the process never stops. From this point on until his death, Wagner, and after him composers like Richard Strauss and Alban Berg, labored to develop a musical expression which more and more exhaustively extends into the powerful realm of musical expression the psychology and the emotion inherent in the dramatic situation. This drive led Wagner to the eventual abandonment of the forms of opera and brought him to the parting of the ways, where it was imperative for him to devise a program whereby he could most consistently and uninhibitedly engage in just this kind of musical-dramatic synthesis. This is at the root of all his experimentation; it is the basis of his theories on the synthesis of arts; it is the need which explains why he was impelled to the construction of those theories and the composition of his revolutionary mature works. It is the beginning of this process that we observe in *The Flying Dutchman*.

The poem is in striking contrast to the poem of *Rienzi*. Somber in mood and simpler in its outline, it offers a much better opportunity for musical intensification than did the gaudier,. showier *Rienzi* text. Wagner claimed much more for it than for the earlier work. "From *The Flying Dutchman* on I begin my career as a poet as I end that of a preparer of opera libretti." (W.S., IV, 266) There is no doubt of its intrinsic superiority to *Rienzi*, although it contains none of the elements Wagner was later to develop to make his word-tone synthesis more complete. As in the earlier opera, the verse form varies from rhymed iambic tetrameters to blank verse, although the proportion of the latter is much increased. There are also a few lines of hexameter.

The musical setting of the dialog varies from the most conventional operatic tradition to experimental word-tone synthesis which heralds the coming *Gesamtkunstwerk*. The choruses are the most conservatively treated; numbers like the spinning song in Act II and the sailors' music in Acts I and III are not much different from the choruses of pre-Wagnerian opera. The chorus is always treated as something separate; it never has any decisive connection with the main action. Even the off-stage choruses of the ghostly Dutchman's crew are conventional.

There are numerous arias, duets, and trios throughout the work which are also quite traditional in their treatment. Sometimes these occur even at points of great dramatic interest, following passages which have exploited the dramatic situation in a rather advanced way. When they do so, they come as a kind of retrogression to the listener who is concentrating his attention on the progressive side of the opera. In such passages the melody is, in the main, independently constructed from a purely musical standpoint, with again only the nominal regard for the poetic accent that has been noted in *Rienzi*. Verse accent gives way to musical contour whenever the two do not coincide. The following example is taken from the beginning of the most important scene of the entire opera, the first meeting between the Dutchman and Senta:

Wohl hub auch ich   voll Sehn-sucht mei - ne Blik - ke
(*I too raised my glance full of longing*

p. 147

aus tie - fer Nacht   em - por ___ zu ei - nem Weib.
out of deepest night to a woman.)

The melody, which divides naturally into four sections of two measures each, is set to two lines of blank verse. Consequently it clashes with the rhythm and accents of the text. The strong accent of the first beat of the measure falls in at least two cases on syllables which should be unstressed ("aus," "empor"). This is true also of the secondary accent of the third beat in the measure (Blick*e*"). The rise and fall of the pitch is not determined by the words, but by the formal design of the melody.

There is a certain amount of the traditional type of operatic recitative:

Mit Schät-zen al - ler Ge -gen-den und Zo - nen ist reich mein Schiff be-
(*With treasures from all realms and regions my ship is richly*

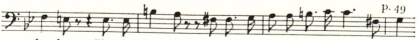

la -den: willst du han - deln, so sollst du si -cher dei-nes Vor - teils sein.
laden: if you wish to bargain, you may be sure of gain.)

p. 49

But there is also more stirring dramatic dialog which gives fuller play to the musical aspect without distorting the rhythm of the poetry:

SENTA

Soll mich des Ärm - sten Schrek-ken-los nicht rüh-ren?
(*Should the fearful fate of the poor man not move me?*)

ERIK

Mein Lei - den, Sen - ta, rührt es dich nicht mehr?
My suffering, Senta, does it not move you more?

SENTA

O, prah - le nicht! Was kann dein Lei -den sein?
Oh, do not boast! What can your suffering be?

p. 129

Kennst je - nes Un-glück-sel' -gen Schick - sal du?
Do you know the fate of that unhappy man?)

Even without the lively orchestral accompaniment supporting it and adding to the emotional intensity, it can be seen that this is a decided departure from the ordinary recitative quoted just above. The fragmentary nature of the melodic lines, interrupted by numerous pauses, heightens the sense of excitement. The accents of the verse are, without exception, carefully calculated in the fashioning of the melodic line. But what is more important, the melodic line itself contributes to the dramatic effect of these accents. The strong emphasis on the word "Schreckenlos" is the result of the gradual rise in pitch from the beginning of the phrase to the first syllable of the word; of the primary accent of the down beat on "Sch*reck*enlos"; and of the sudden, sharp plunge to deeper tones on the second and third syllables, with the break closely following. All these separate factors conduce to a more powerful emotional interpretation of the word.

The balance of accents in "O, prahle nicht," in the second line, is minutely calculated: the "O" is on the down beat, and the ordinarily weaker accent of the third beat on "prahle" is strengthened by virtue of the pause which immediately precedes it. The natural tendency of a stronger beat on "O" and a weaker on "prahle" is also counteracted by the relative importance of the pitches. "O" is placed on the submediant, which gives it the feeling of an upbeat to the strong dominant of "prahle." This strengthening is completed by the extension of the note for one and a half beats.

Similarly, the stress of "mein" and the parallel stress of "dein" are obtained by placing them on the down beat and by extending the note for two full beats in each case. On its first occurrence, "Leiden" receives a stress by virtue of its position on the third beat, as well as by the fact that the high pitch is maintained. At its repetition by Senta, there is no need for such emphasis, and the pitch is therefore lower, so that in this instance the stress falls on "dein" as required by the declamation. The downward course of the melody in the last phrase, "jenes Unglücksel'gen Schicksal," is designed to strengthen the tragic nature of the words. This type of passage is clearly a forerunner of the dramatic dialog in the *Gesamtkunstwerk* of *Opera and Drama*.

In the main, as Guido Adler points out, Wagner's most successful advances toward a *Gesamtkunstwerk* in the *The Flying Dutchman* are in those sections where he is extending existing forms and infusing into them something characteristically Wagnerian, filling them fuller of emotional power than had hitherto been the case. Of these the two outstanding examples are Senta's ballad and the long monolog of the Dutchman in Act I. In the most "advanced" section of the opera, Eric's dream narrative in Act II, he was less successful. Here is a first attempt at the kind of dramatic writing which appears again in Tannhäuser's Rome narrative, in the Grail narrative at the close of *Lohengrin*, and reaches sublimity in the great narrative of Isolde in Act I of *Tristan and Isolde*. But the dream narrative in *The Flying Dutchman* has neither the color of the best arias nor the dramatic interest of the best recitatives. It is a poetic-musical synthesis in its way, but it is relatively barren and fails to sustain the interest. Wagner had not yet found the secret of this kind of writing.

The orchestra in its harmonic support of the arias and recitatives is richer in texture, if less noisy, than it was in *Rienzi*. This is a step toward the function of the orchestra in the mature works, but still a preliminary one, for the harmonic integration does not extend to the individual phrases as it does in the later works. The chief advance in the function of the orchestra is in the matter of leitmotif, which plays an increasingly important part in each succeeding work of this period, though again in this instance there is a world of difference between the tentative experimentation in the pre-*Opera and Drama* works and the wealth of invention and systematic use of leitmotif in the *Ring* dramas. In *The Flying Dutchman* the leitmotif which most clearly foreshadows the motif of reminiscence of the later works is the Redemption motif, sung by Senta in the famous ballad. It has this·effect principally because it is drawn from a melodic line and as a consequence always recalls a conceptual idea when it is later repeated:

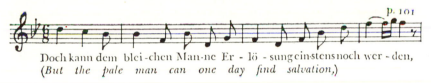

p. 101

Doch kann dem blei-chen Man-ne Er - lö - sung einstens noch wer - den,
(*But the pale man can one day find salvation,*)

The other motifs, the open fifth of the Dutchman, the surging motif of the sea, or the lilting folk-song-like motif of the Norwegian sailors, rely rather on their musical descriptive power, since they are not drawn from a melodic line and therefore on their reappearance do not recall a specific verse. The Redemption motif appears at nine different points in the action and, at each repetition with or without words, is used to include the idea of redemption at the moment of its being played or sung. Thus, for instance, it is played by the orchestra beneath a vocal line by the Dutchman, when he first realizes Senta's willingness to sacrifice her life for him:

p. 158

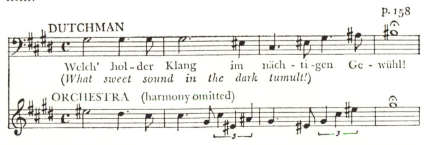

DUTCHMAN

Welch' hol-der Klang im näch - ti-gen Ge - wühl!
(*What sweet sound in the dark tumult!*)

ORCHESTRA (harmony omitted)

The melody alone, played by the orchestra, is sufficient to add the connotation of redemption to the thought of the words sung by the Dutchman, because the first appearance of this melody has been associated with the words of Senta in the ballad. In this way, the inner meaning of the Dutchman's words is revealed by the music. This is very much like the motif of reminiscence, the program for which is set forth in *Opera and Drama*. It is the only one in *The Flying Dutchman*.

But there are other novel ways in which Wagner uses leitmotif in this work. In the two strikingly contrasting motifs of the Dutchman and Redemption Wagner had material ready made for dramatic underlining of the stage situation, and in a number of scenes he uses one or the other or both with telling effect. In the great scene between Senta and the Dutchman in the second act, there is a moment when the Dutchman theme is heard, followed immediately by the opening bars of that part of Senta's ballad to which she had sung the words, "Ach, wann wirst du, bleicher Seemann, sie finden?" ("Ah, when will you, pale seaman, find her?"). Similarly, at the end of their first duet, in which the Dutchman is questioning whether Senta is the heaven-sent one who will remain true to him, and Senta is joyfully anticipating the fulfillment of her longing to redeem the Dutchman through her faithfulness, there sounds in the orchestra once more the jubilant theme which was first heard at the end of Senta's ballad, when she burst forth with her ecstatic "Durch mich sollst du das Heil erreichen!" ("Through me shall you attain salvation!"). These are clear foreshadowings of things to come.

chapter five

Tannhäuser

THE TWO WAGNERS are present in *Tannhäuser* as well, but in this work the later Wagner is proportionately much more in evidence and his hand is a surer one.* Certain traditional elements which are still relatively unchanged carry with them the strongest intimation of grand opera. The chorus parts, the septet in Scene 2 of Act I, and the duet between Tannhäuser and Elisabeth in Act II are the most prominent of these. A superficial glance through the score might lead one to believe that *Tannhäuser* is quite in the usual operatic vein. A quick comparison with the *Ring* dramas would strengthen that opinion, for there is still a long way to go from *Tannhäuser* to *The Rhinegold*. But a careful study reveals the thoroughness with which the spirit of the later Wagner pervades it.

In this regard, the long account "On the Performance of Tannhäuser," which Wagner wrote for the benefit of directors and actors, is of interest. It was written in 1852, to be sure, and reflects to some extent the further stage of development Wagner had reached by that time, but it is also a revealing document on the opera. The most striking thing about the essay is the degree to which Wagner asks that the musical be subordinated to the dramatic in actual performance. "If I am so fortunate as to be correctly understood by the singers," he writes, "with regard to the proper manner of delivery, and if this has been thoroughly assimilated by them, then finally I urge that the strict observance of the musical beat be given up almost completely. For up to this point it has served as a mechanical aid whereby the composer and the singer

---

* I discuss in this chapter the original, or Dresden, version (1845), not the later revision, known as the Paris version (1861).

reach an understanding. Once this mutual understanding has been achieved, however, it can be discarded as a worn-out, useless and moreover bothersome tool. Let the singer give absolutely free rein to his natural feeling, yes, even to the physical necessities of his breathing in the more agitated phrases, and the more creative he can become through the fullest freedom of emotion, the more he will earn my most grateful thanks." (W.S., V, 129) This is quite clearly a plea to let the rhythm and nuances of the dialog be the determining factor in the final stages.

In the same essay, Wagner makes an urgent plea for the correct delivery of the repeated phrase "Erbarm dich mein" ("Have mercy on me") in the long ensemble at the end of Act II, in the following terms: "To every future Tannhäuser goes my plea to give most particular attention to this passage. His delivery of it will be successful only if he is fully conscious of dominating the dramatic as well as the musical situation. . . . The cries 'Have mercy on me!' demand such a piercing accent that the Tannhäuser who is no more than a well trained singer will not succeed. Rather the highest dramatic art must provide him with the energy of grief and despair for the expression, which must seem to burst forth from the depths of a fearfully suffering heart like a cry for redemption." (W.S., V, 135)

In the adjustment of music to word in the dramatic dialog Wagner has made important strides. The verse and the melodic line do not clash with one another in *Tannhäuser*. To be sure, they are blended with varying degrees of success and care, but severe distortion of verse accent by a formal melodic line occurs in only one number. The proportion between formal numbers and declamatory recitative (which assumes a form very prophetic of the mature Wagner) shows for the first time a preponderance of the latter. Even the arias reflect a considerable degree of care for synchronizing poetic and musical rhythm. Sharp division into a succession of concerted pieces with intervening recitative gives way to a more fluid transition which points toward *Lohengrin*. Where a series of independent numbers does occur, as at the beginning of the third act, there is an excellent dramatic justification, and the separate components are not felt as operatic numbers in the traditional sense, for the duration of which one must perforce suspend his sense of the dramatic situation. Each represents a definite step in the dramatic development.

"In my opera," wrote Wagner in 1852 in the aforementioned essay, "there is no difference between so-called 'declaimed' and 'sung' phrases, but rather my declamation is song and my song declamation. The definite cessation of 'song' and the definite commencement of the usual 'recitative,' by virtue of which the delivery of the singers is divided into two quite distinct manners, does not occur in my work." (W.S., V, 128) Since *Tannhäuser* is a transitional work, it does not exhibit the homogeneity of style that marks the later works, and with these in mind one might be tempted to discredit Wagner's remark as an exaggeration. But it is literally true and should be considered with reference to the earlier works, not the later ones, which did not yet exist when he wrote these words.

The verse form is nominally rhymed or unrhymed iambic tetrameter, pentameter or hexameter, with a few trimeters, alternating quite freely. Actually, there is a great deal of free verse, thinly disguised as one of the standard meters. In general, regular rhymed verse is used for the more formal parts, those most closely related to traditional opera, and free verse for the dramatic recitative, of which the following is an example:

> Die Zeit, die hier ich verweil', ich kann sie nicht
> ermessen!—Tage, Monde gibt's für mich
> nicht mehr, denn nicht mehr sehe ich die Sonne,
> nicht mehr des Himmels freundliche Gestirne;—
> den Halm seh' ich nicht mehr, der frisch ergrünend,
> den neuen Sommer bringt;—die Nachtigall
> hör' ich nicht mehr, die mir den Lenz verkünde!
> Hör' ich sie nie, seh' ich sie niemals mehr? *

Even when spoken, these lines could hardly be delivered as pentameter. When set to Wagner's melodic line (see below), they lose all vestige of such a character. This kind of verse presages his rejection in *Opera and Drama* of all formal rhythmic patterns. The other principles of versification which he formulated in that work

---

* *Tannhäuser*, vocal score, p. 30. The lines also appear in W.S., II, 5 with slight alterations. It is never safe to rely on the words of any of the dramas as printed in the *Sämtliche Schriften*. Sometimes, as here, the differences are almost negligible; sometimes they are considerable.

and carried out in the *Ring* poems are not anticipated in *Tannhäuser*.

The very first pages of poetic-musical dialog show the gulf separating *Tannhäuser* from Wagner's previous works. The verse and the melody fit perfectly, the natural accent of the verse is the governing factor in the formation of the melody. The melody has intrinsic emotional and dramatic beauty, and this beauty is so devised as to supplement the content of the verse. There is nothing tentative any longer about this word-tone amalgamation. The lines quoted above are set to music thus:

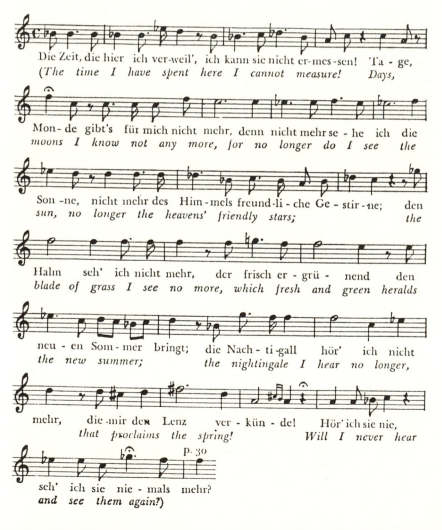

Die Zeit, die hier ich ver-weil', ich kann sie nicht er-mes-sen! Ta - ge,
(*The time I have spent here I cannot measure! Days,*

Mon- de gibt's für mich nicht mehr, denn nicht mehr se - he ich die
moons I know not any more, for no longer do I see the

Son -ne, nicht mehr des Him - mels freund-li - che Ge - stir -ne; den
sun, no longer the heavens' friendly stars; the

Halm seh' ich nicht mehr, der frisch er - grü - nend den
blade of grass I see no more, which fresh and green heralds

neu - en Som- mer bringt; die Nach - ti -gall hör' ich nicht
the new summer; the nightingale I hear no longer,

mehr, die -mir den Lenz ver - kün - de! Hör' ich sie nie,
that proclaims the spring! Will I never hear

p. 30

seh' ich sie nie - mals mehr?
and see them again?)

In spite of the rather pronounced tendency to a dotted rhythm, the melody divides the verse into the thought and breath groups which would result if the verses were spoken, and yields the following free pattern:

Die Zeit, die hier ich verweil',
ich kann sie nicht ermessen!
Tage, Monde gibt's für mich nicht mehr,
denn nicht mehr sehe ich die Sonne,
nicht mehr des Himmels freundliche Gestirne;
den Halm seh' ich nicht mehr,
der frisch ergrünend, den neuen Sommer bringt,
die Nachtigall hör' ich nicht mehr,
die mir den Lenz verkünde!
Hör' ich sie nie,
seh' ich sie niemals mehr?

In the arias, word and tone are not so minutely blended, but even the most formal melodic patterns are designed to fit the words:

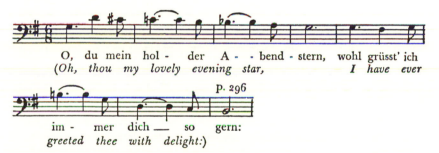

O, du mein hol - der A - - bend - stern, wohl grüsst' ich
(Oh, thou my lovely evening star, I have ever

p. 296

im - mer dich — so gern:
greeted thee with delight:)

The parallel construction of the melody in this aria requires the exact repetition of the first four bars of melody. This would cause distortion of the rhythm of the verse, but is avoided by giving over the exact repetition to the cellos. The vocal line is varied to suit the natural accents of the poetry:

VOICE

p. 297

Vom Her- zen, das sie nie — ver - riet,
(From the heart which remained faithful to her,)

CELLOS

With the exception of these four bars the orchestra plays only harp-like accompanying arpeggios. This "Evening Star" is the most formal aria in *Tannhäuser*. All the others are freer and make bolder adaptations of melody to verse.

There is one exception, the duet between Tannhäuser and Elisabeth in Act II, "Gepriesen sei die Stunde" ("Praised be the hour"). For the length of this number we are in traditional grand opera again. In view of the advanced nature of the rest of the work, this is a surprising interlude:

Von Won - - - ne - glanz   um - ge - - ben lacht
(*In ecstatic splendor the sun's glow smiles upon me,*)

p. 119

mir der Son - ne Schein,

At highly dramatic moments there occur some thrilling examples of musical-poetic or mimetic-musical synthesis, clearly foreshadowing the Wagner to come. One of the most electrifying moments is in the first act. Tannhäuser refuses to return to the Wartburg. The entreaties of his friends become more and more impassioned, and his denials more and more firm, until the ensemble breaks off suddenly as Wolfram invokes the name of Elisabeth, with an overpowering effect on Tannhäuser:

WOLFRAM

TANNHÄUSER
(Heftig und freudig ergriffen)
(in violent and joyful agitation)
p. 76

Bleib' bei E - li - sa beth!   E - li - sa - beth!
(*Stay with Elizabeth!*   *Elizabeth!*)

The climax is dramatic, not musical. It is brought about by the name, and the effect of this name on Tannhäuser. The line is not striking musically. The principal effect of the musical setting is to extend the vowel, thereby prolonging the climactic moment and intensifying the emotional effect. This is an excellent antecedent example of an important principle worked out later in *Opera and Drama*.

Another example in which the musical note is used to prolong and intensify the dramatic effect of the word with which it is sung is the following:

WOLFRAM   TANNHÄUSER (wütend)
                                                      (furious)

Zogst du denn nicht nach Rom? ⇗ Schweig' —— mir von
(*Did you not go to Rome?*)   *Be silent about Rome!*

WOLFRAM   TANNHÄUSER

Rom! ⇗ Warst nicht beim heil-'gen Fe - ste? ⇗ Schweig' ——
      Were you not at the holy festival?   *Be silent*

p. 302

—— mir von ihm!
about it!)

The most famous precursor of the later Wagnerian synthesis is Tannhäuser's narrative in the final act. Almost two hundred measures long, it is the most extended piece of dramatic recitative in all the works preceding *Opera and Drama*. It contains, in germ at least, more of the details of organic synthesis than any other. The focus of attention is the narrative itself. There is no extraneous melodic pattern. The construction of the melody is based on the words to which it is attached. There is coincidence of accent throughout. All the emotional power of the music is centered on the narrative, as it builds up gradually to a shattering climax. In this narrative, the character of the melodic line changes with every shift of ideas in the verse. In *The Flying Dutchman* the musical intensification of mood was on broad lines only. It did not extend to individual words and phrases, to short, rapid changes of emphasis, as it does now in Tannhäuser's narrative.

As it begins ("Inbrunst im Herzen"), the music expresses the devoutness of heart which Tannhäuser felt as he began his journey to Rome. In the sixth bar, the thought turns to Elisabeth ("Ein

Engel hatte, ach!"), and the character of the melodic line changes to express Elisabeth's angelic innocence, with a suggestion of the tragedy Tannhäuser has brought into her life. Thirteen measures later, the music again changes as the narrative turns to the pilgrims ("schwerstbedrückte Pilger") who are journeying to Rome. Tannhäuser has joined them and next describes, in four pairs of verses, the contrast between the comparative comfort of the others during their pilgrimage, and his own self-imposed mortifications:

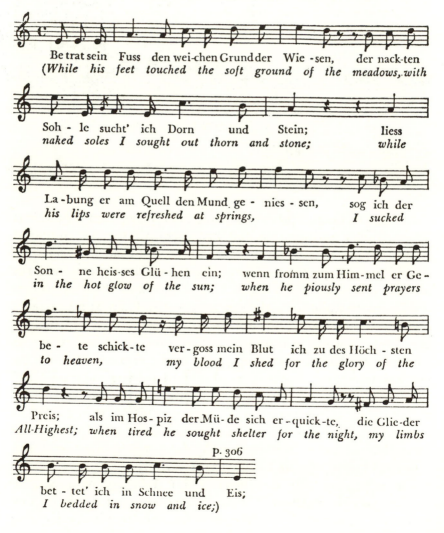

Be trat sein Fuss den wei-chen Grund der Wie -sen, der nack-ten
(While his feet touched the soft ground of the meadows, with

Soh - le sucht' ich Dorn und Stein; liess
naked soles I sought out thorn and stone; while

La -bung er am Quell den Mund ge - nies - sen, sog ich der
his lips were refreshed at springs, I sucked

Son - ne heis-ses Glü - hen ein; wenn fromm zum Him-mel er Ge -
in the hot glow of the sun; when he piously sent prayers

be - te schick-te ver - goss mein Blut ich zu des Höch - sten
to heaven, my blood I shed for the glory of the

Preis; als im Hos - piz der Mü- de sich er -quick-te, die Glie-der
All-Highest; when tired he sought shelter for the night, my limbs

p. 306

bet - tet' ich in Schnee und Eis;
I bedded in snow and ice;)

The configuration of the melodic line strengthens the contrasts. The first half of each of the sections is brighter than the second, in exact accord with the sense of the verse. The actual contour of the lines of the first sections is more straightforward, involving simpler harmonies, with a good proportion of bright major chords. In the alternating sections, the contour is more involved, with somber minor and diminished seventh harmonies. In each case, too, the first half lies in a higher vocal register, which fact also adds to the contrast. The changes are subtle and carefully proportioned to fit the nature of the narrative. The orchestral accompaniment contributes a good deal to the effect by its constant modulation from one key to another, a further characteristic of the later Wagner which appears for the first time in *Tannhäuser*. What follows this quoted section for nine measures expresses the dark hues of Tannhäuser's contrition, and on the tenth measure there is again a sudden brightening as he once more thinks of his "angel." This description has covered only one fourth of the narrative. Such detailed interplay between word and tone goes on throughout the entire passage.

A prominent feature of the later works making its first appearance in *Tannhäuser* is the melodic pictorialization of individual words, the device of paralleling in the music the import of a single descriptive word. It is of course not claimed that this is new with Wagner. There are many stunning examples in earlier music, particularly in the cantatas of Bach. It is not discussed as a separate entity in *Opera and Drama,* or in any of Wagner's theory, but it plays a large part in his works, and it is an effective means of word-tone amalgamation. The pictorializations in *Tannhäuser* are not as audacious as those which come later, but they deserve notice as preliminary manifestations. There are only about a dozen of them altogether. Five of them are quoted here:

zog   ju - - - - belnd
(*went   jubilantly*)

The chord was sketched into the second example because the effect of dullness on the word "matt" is obtained by the C of the melody, which adds a hollow sounding minor ninth to the dominant seventh chord beneath it. The third example needs the complete poetic line to explain the downward plunge of the minor arpeggio on the word "jubelnd," giving it an ominous quality quite opposite from the meaning of the word. Elisabeth is addressing the knights in Act II:

> Seht mich, die Jungfrau . . .
> der *jubelnd* er das Herz zerstach.
>
> (See me, the maid . . .
> Whose heart he *jubilantly* pierced.)

Contrast the dark sound of this descending minor line with the joyful ascending arpeggio on the same word in the first example, which has no tragic undertone. The accompaniment was included in the last two examples, because it contributes importantly to the total effect. But it is to be noted that the melodic verse itself contains the essential pictorialization. It is not primarily orchestral. This is important because it accords with Wagner's later principle that the melodic verse itself must be the "life-giving center" of the dramatic structure.

I have already alluded to the role of the orchestra several times. It is gradually moving into the orbit of the musical dialog. In *Tannhäuser* it executes the modulations which the melodic line requires. It assists in the pictorializations. By appropriate harmonies, it increases the force of the changes in musical mood to coincide with changes in the concepts embodied in the verse. The use of leitmotif is not strikingly different from that in *The Flying Dutchman*. There are occasional effective repetitions by the orchestra of a melodic line with a specific previous connotation. In Act II, when the Landgrave mentions the return of Tannhäuser, the melody which had been sung by Wolfram in Act I to the words, "War's Wunder, war es reine Macht" ("Was it a miracle, was it the power of purity"), referring to Elisabeth's power over Tannhäuser, is heard in the orchestra. In the prelude to Act III, written as a musical portrayal of Tannhäuser's journey to Rome, there is an interweaving of various motifs which is prophetic of the later much more elaborate leitmotif technique. But there is no motif which functions as did the Redemption motif in *The Flying Dutchman* as a precursor of the motif of reminiscence.

Considered as a step toward the *Gesamtkunstwerk*, *Tannhäuser*'s most significant advance is in the increased shift of emphasis from the traditional operatic forms to the dramatic dialog. *Lohengrin* will carry this tendency even farther. In that opera, we will find musical dialog in which the musical aspect is subordinated more rigidly to the poetic delivery than in any other work of Wagner's.

chapter six

Lohengrin

"NOWHERE in the score of my *Lohengrin* have I written the word 'recitative'; the singers are not to know that there are recitatives in it. On the contrary, I have made an effort to calculate the speech rhythm so exactly and sharply that the singers need only sing the notes exactly in accordance with their note values and the rhythm will be correct." (W.L., I, 79) Thus Wagner in a letter to Franz Liszt during the latter's preparation for the first performance of *Lohengrin* in Weimar. We will have occasion to see that the work itself is not as radically different from traditional opera as one might assume from the above statement. Yet it is very true that in major portions of *Lohengrin* the speech rhythm is the determining element for the melodic-poetic combination. In certain passages this principle is carried through so rigorously that the melodic aspect plays a more subordinate role than in any other of Wagner's works.

Lohengrin's narrative in Act III is a perfect example, and a comparison of it with Tannhäuser's (see p. 46) shows clearly the difference in the relationship of poetry and music. Whereas in Tannhäuser's narrative one finds elaborate harmonic accompaniment, modulation, and functional extension of vowel sound, in Lohengrin's only one of these devices, vowel extension, occurs, and that in a much modified form. Normal speech rhythm is the factor which dominates all others:

All - jähr - lich naht vom Him-mel ei - ne Tau - be, um
(Each year there approaches from heaven a dove, to

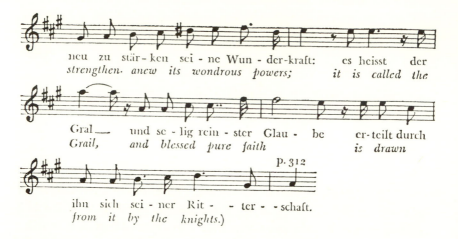

neu   zu   stär - ken   sei - ne   Wun - der-kraft: es   heisst   der
strengthen. anew   its   wondrous   powers;   *it   is   called   the*

Gral___   und   se - lig   rein - ster   Glau -   be   er-teilt durch
Grail,   *and   blessed   pure   faith*   *is   drawn*

p. 312

ihn   sich   sei - ner   Rit - - ter - - schaft.
from   it   by   the   knights.)

The rhythm of the melody and the contour of the melodic line
accommodate themselves as perfectly to the declamatory aspect of
the poetic verse as it is possible for music to do. There is musical
interest in the melodic line, but decidedly less than in Tannhäuser's narrative. The accompaniment is also much simpler. The
entire narrative is sung either to tremolo chords or to the theme of
the Holy Grail. There is no harmonic elucidation, no modulation,
no pictorialization.

In the less dramatic moments of the opera, there is sometimes
even less importance to the vocal line and orchestral accompaniment. Compare the following, taken from the early pages of the
score, with the example from the beginning of *Tannhäuser* (on
p. 42):

Lust - wan-delnd führ - te   El - sa   den   Kna-ben   einst   zum
(On   a   stroll   one   day   Elsa   led   the   boy   to   a   wood,

Wald,   doch   oh - ne   ihn   kehr-te   sie   zu-rück;   mit   fal-scher Sor-ge
but   without   him   she   returned;   with   feigned   concern   she

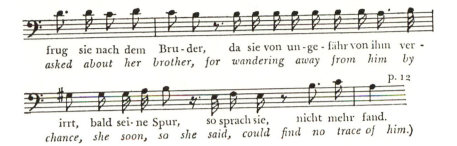

frug sie nach dem Bru - der, da sie von un - ge - fähr von ihm ver -
asked about her brother, for wandering away from him by

irrt, bald sei - ne Spur, so sprach sie, nicht mehr fand.
chance, she soon, so she said, could find no trace of him.)

p. 12

Low tremolo chords in the strings are the sole accompaniment to
this musical-poetic line: an F major chord in the beginning, changing to F minor at "Wald," to a diminished seventh (G♯, B, D, F,)
at "zurück," and to a dominant seventh on E at "verirrt." This cannot be called harmonic elucidation. The melodic line adheres
rigidly to the declamatory accent, but it is of negligible significance. The musical participation could hardly be cut down to a
barer minimum.

In fact, although they are not labelled so, numerous passages
like the above are reminiscent of the recitative of pre-Wagnerian
opera. But this does not actually indicate a retrogression on
Wagner's part, because these passages are the result of his effort
to make the dialog consistently the center of attention. He had not
yet learned how to sustain the interest at the points in his drama
where there is least tension and excitement and occasionally fell
into a style very nearly like recitative. Yet even here the delivery
is much richer, more full-bodied and vigorous than in traditional
recitative. Indeed, such inevitable moments in any dramatic action
are the least successful passages even in Wagner's greatest works.
But when the dramatic interest and psychological tension are high,
the musical-dramatic dialog is dynamic and forceful in a way that
traditional opera cannot be. The long scene between Ortrud and
Telramund at the opening of Act II is the finest example of this
and the most advanced writing done by Wagner up to this time.

A striking confirmation of this assertion that Wagner was subordinating the music to the words at this period more fully than at
any other time in his career exists in the fragment of an orchestra

sketch he made of the first scene of *Siegfried's Death* in 1850. This
is the only operatic composing he did in the five years between
the completion of *Lohengrin* in 1848 and the beginning of *The
Rhinegold* in 1853. It exhibits the same rigid suppression of
musical expression we have been discussing in *Lohengrin*. The
excerpt is so colorless that we can only be glad Wagner did not go
on with the composition at that time. From the 162-measure sketch,
which was published for the first time in *L'Illustration* February
11, 1933, the following is an eighteen-bar excerpt:

ERSTE NORN

Der Göt-ter Burg bau-ten   Rie - sen,   be - gehr-ten
(*The gods' fortress giants built,   and demanded with*

dro - hend zum Dank den   Ring.   Ihn ent - ris -sen die Göt-ter dem
threats as reward the ring.   The gods wrested it from

ZWEITE NORN

Ni - be-lung.   Sor - gen seh   ich die Göt - ter,   es
the Nibelung.   Troubled are the gods,   in

grollt   in Ban - den die Tie - fe.   Frei - e nur ge - ben
bondage the depths grumble.   Free ones alone bring

DRITTE NORN

Frie-den. ⁼ Freu-dig trot-zet ein Fro - her,   frei für die Got-ter zu
peace.   Joyfully defiant a happy one is free to fight for

strei - ten, durch Sieg bringt Frie - de ein Held!
the gods, by victory a hero will bring peace!)

One need only compare this with the scene as it was ultimately composed in *Twilight of the Gods* to see what a world of development lay in between. Even when compared to the musical dialog of *The Rhinegold*, which is the first music to follow it in point of time of composition, there is a noticeable difference in poetic-musical balance.

In *Lohengrin,* not all of the musical dialog is of this kind, however. There is a good deal of formal melody, as illustrated by the following:

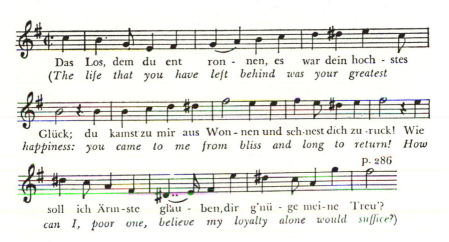

Das Los, dem du ent ron - nen, es war dein hoch - stes
(*The life that you have left behind was your greatest*

Glück; du kamst zu mir aus Won - nen und seh nest dich zu -ruck! Wie
happiness: you came to me from bliss and long to return! How

p. 286

soll ich Ärm-ste glau - ben, dir g'nü - ge mei-ne Treu'?
can I, poor one, believe my loyalty alone would suffice?)

In a certain mechanical sense, this excerpt does accord with normal speech rhythm, as Wagner claimed in his letter to Liszt, but in a more important sense, it does not. The lines are sung by Elsa at a moment of great tension, just before she loses control of herself completely and asks Lohengrin the forbidden question. The melody, however, does not express this intensity, nor does it cling closely to the verse; it has a pattern of its own which is worked out in full and which would make good musical sense even as an orchestra melody without words. Consequently, attention is drawn away from the words to the music, which is here in a way in competition with the text.

This kind of formal musical phrase occurs often and in all parts of the drama. Many other examples could be cited. Below is part of King Henry's prayer from Act I:

Des Rei - nen Arm gib_ Hel-den- kraft,   des Fal -schen
(*To the pure one's arm give heroic power; may the*

p-77

Stär -ke sei   er - schlafft:___
false one's strength fail:)

Such passages as these are also not to be thought of as reversions to a pre-Wagnerian state, any more than are the recitative-like passages discussed above. They are far from being arias. In *Lohengrin* Wagner has made the dramatic dialog so consistently the center of attention that there are almost no set pieces in the traditional sense. Even in such passages as these, which most nearly approach the pre-Wagnerian dominance of the melodic line over the verse, the dramatic situation remains fluid and transitional. There is nothing in *Lohengrin* like the beginning of Act III of *Tannhäuser*, for instance, where Wolfram's recitative, the chorus of pilgrims, Elisabeth's prayer, and Wolfram's "Evening Star" aria form four distinct units which do not overlap. The fact that there are fewer excerpts from *Lohengrin* than from *Tannhäuser* which can be performed in concert stems from this. Even Elsa's dream, the most frequently heard, must be adapted, for its three parts are separated in the opera by interludes of which the second is no less than eighty-six measures long.

Robert Schumann was worried about the lack of clearly defined subdivisions when Wagner gave a private reading of the poem to some friends in Dresden in 1845, and Wagner, who of course was not deterred or perturbed by such conservative criticism, reports that he read it to him over again with tongue in cheek, arbitrarily dividing it into "arias," "duets," "recitatives," etc. on the spur of the moment. According to Wagner, all Schumann's misgivings were allayed when he heard it read this way.

Still, though the passages we have been discussing cannot be considered as arias, being more fragmentary and more closely integrated into the flow of the dialog, they do share with the aria the formal melodic line. We see in them, then, the final vestiges of traditional operatic form, modified to accord with the new focus of attention. In *The Rhinegold,* his next work, Wagner makes a clean break with operatic tradition.

The meter of the *Lohengrin* poem is more regular than in *Tannhäuser,* and there are many more rhymed lines. There is little of the kind of free verse we noted in the earlier poem. Such regular rhymed lines may have been a factor in causing Wagner to use formal melody, even though for more basic reasons he was drawing away from this kind of composing. The poem exhibits two new features which are significant in the light of what was to come. It has touches of archaisms and some alliteration, most of the latter in Elsa's opening narrative, known as Elsa's dream ("Einsam in trüben Tagen"). Wagner was apparently quite proud of these innovations and makes much of them in his "Communication to my Friends," where he writes, "In *Lohengrin* I observed an even greater fidelity than in *Tannhäuser* in the presentation of the historical-legendary elements, through which alone such an unusual subject could be convincingly portrayed to the senses. This prompted me to proceed in the scenic representation and the expression of the dialog in a direction in which I later was led to the discovery of possibilities which in order to be consistent demanded a completely novel adjustment of the factors of operatic expression." (W.S., IV, 300) Their intrinsic importance in *Lohengrin,* however, as contrasted with their significance as indications of what the future was to hold, is slight.

In the matter of leitmotif and the more complex form of motif of reminiscence, *Lohengrin* occupies an intermediary position between *Tannhäuser* and *The Rhinegold.* In the earlier work we have seen that there were no leitmotifs which could be designated as forerunners of the *Opera and Drama* motif of reminiscence; in *The Rhinegold* the greater proportion of the motifs are genuine examples of this. *Lohengrin* contains an approximately equal proportion of both types. The "Verbot" motif, the central one of the drama, originating in the poetic-melodic line, is a direct anticipation of *Opera and Drama:*

Nie sollst du mich be - fra - gen,   noch Wis-sens Sor-ge tra-gen, wo
(Never shall you ask me,   nor be concerned to know

her ich kam der Fahrt,— noch wie mein Nam' und Art!
whence I have come,   nor my name and lineage!)

It is of interest to note that for melodic purposes the word "noch" must bear an emphasis which it is not important enough to warrant. Wagner was apparently conscious of this discrepancy. While he has added weight to the entire first half of the phrase by the unusual expedient of putting a stress mark over each note, he carefully omits the mark over "noch." This is, of course, not sufficient to prevent it from receiving a very strong accent by virtue of its position on the strongest beat of the measure and at the beginning of the answer to the opening phrase.

This motif occurs soon after Lohengrin's entrance in Act I and does not recur in that act, there being no further occasion for its use. The mental conflict this "Verbot" arouses in Elsa, which is the central theme of the drama, begins only in Act II. Here, the motif appears seven times, and in Act III, five times. Of these, it appears eight times in the orchestra alone, each time for the purpose of a distinct emotional reminiscence, linking the vocal line or the stage action with which it occurs to the words, "Nie sollst du mich befragen!" Most effective is its repetition at the close of Act II. At this point, to all external appearances, the uncertainties which have been aroused in Elsa's mind by Ortrud and Friedrich have been dispelled by Lohengrin. But the fact that their plan has actually had its effect on her is revealed by the pointed announcement of the motif, by trumpets and trombones, accompanied by the following stage action: "With timid concern [Elsa] glances . . . to the right and downward and catches sight of Ortrud, who raises her arm toward Elsa, as though certain of victory. Elsa turns away terrified . . . the curtain falls." (*Lohengrin*, 255) In a letter to Liszt (September 8, 1850) Wagner laid great stress on the im-

portance of coordinating the action with the announcement of
the motif at this point. And well he might! He had heard that during the first performance of *Lohengrin* in Weimar under Liszt's
direction, the curtain had already fallen before the motif sounded!

Most striking use of motif of reminiscence in all pre-*Opera
and Drama* Wagner is that in Act II, where Ortrud begins her
scheme of planting the seeds of doubt in Elsa's mind. The motif
appears in the orchestra, and, accommodated to the verse, in the
voice as well and injects of course a forceful reminiscence of
Lohengrin's warning at this crucial turning point:

Könn - test du er - fas - sen, wie des - sen
(If you could fathom his nature

Art so wun - der - sam, der nie dich mö - ge so ver -
so strange, so that he would never leave

las - sen, wie er durch Zau - ber zu dir kam!
you miraculously as he came to you!)

p. 151

Wagner's treatment of the chorus in *Lohengrin* is unique in all
his works. For one thing, there is more of it than in any other, although only slightly more in proportion to the length of the work
than in *Tannhäuser*. But more indicative of a new technique is

the frequency of entrances. There are sixty-seven separate choral entrances in *Lohengrin* as against twenty-four in *Tannhäuser*. As this comparison indicates, the *Lohengrin* chorus is integrated more fully into the action. It takes a more significant part in the proceedings, especially at moments of dramatic climax, where it often participates in the dialog, injecting brief exclamations and comments of only several measures' duration. There is here a clear attempt to break up the stereotype of a mass of singers on the stage who hover at the periphery of the action and sing only occasionally in concerted numbers.

Yet the attempt is only partially successful, chiefly because in addition to the kind of singing just described, Wagner has given over many pages to the more traditional kind of operatic choral writing, where one or two phrases of text are repeated over and over and an extended choral number develops. This is true particularly in the finale to Act I and of course the "Bridal Chorus." In no work of Wagner, with the exception of *The Mastersingers*, can it be said that he has succeeded in bringing the chorus convincingly into the main action. Indeed, after *Lohengrin*, Wagner dispenses with a chorus entirely until *The Mastersingers* except for a very few measures in the first act of *Tristan and Isolde*.

chapter seven

The Art-Work of the Future

WE HAVE SEEN how Wagner's powerful drive to express the psychology and emotion of his characters more fully than was possible with traditional means impelled him to depart from the traditions of operatic writing. This gradually brought the abandonment of those musical forms and a concentration on the dialog, the moving of which to a more and more central position we have observed in the progression of his three operas. It is entirely consistent with this that Wagner in the later forties should entertain the idea of dispensing with music and trying his hand at pure dialog. From 1846 until at least 1848, he lived with the project of a spoken drama on Frederick Barbarossa, and soon thereafter made extensive preliminary sketches for a *Jesus of Nazareth,* which he intended as a spoken play, possibly with musical background or interludes. This, then, can be considered the extreme point of his development away from opera and toward spoken drama. Neither of these projects was ever carried out. After 1849 came a return to the problems of musical-dramatic synthesis and the admission of the importance of music in his artistic life, although of course it does not imply a return to the abandoned forms. Instead, there is from now on a continual experimentation and wrestling with the idea of a synthesis, both in theory and in practice. It is of interest, however, to observe the manner in which this develops, for there is in both a gradual shift in the relative importance of the music, an adjustment which consistently and increasingly returns the attention more and more to the musical aspect of the synthesis. This process extends throughout the rest of Wagner's life.

The flight of the political fugitive from Dresden into exile in Switzerland in 1849 came just at the time that he was ready to make a clean break with the past artistically as well as politically. The time and psychological circumstances were now ripe for a thorough reckoning, a stock-taking and an attempt to formulate with more precision what had hitherto been aimed at intuitively. That Wagner had broken with the past and resolutely set his gaze forward is abundantly evident in the two essays, *Art and Revolution* (1849), and *The Art-Work of the Future* (1850), whose very titles are sufficient indication of their general tendency. Upon these followed another more detailed and much longer essay, *Opera and Drama* (1851), in which the actual blueprint for Wagner's subsequent artistic production appeared.

The Art-Work of the Future has two main themes. It proclaims the doctrine of an art of the people, by the people, and for the people, an art which would necessarily appeal to the masses because it was an expression of their own thought, feelings and aspirations, a *Gesamtkunstwerk* in a political and social sense; and it portrays a work of art which is the product of a fusion of the separate phases of art, a rebirth of Greek tragedy in modern terms, a synthesis in which the individual phases contribute each in its own way to the total effect, a *Gesamtkunstwerk* in an esthetic sense.

Both of these themes are of course a part of the heritage of Romanticism, and indeed much of Wagner's idealization of the folk sounds like Herder or Rousseau, while his glorification of art as "the satisfaction of the life-need in life itself" (W.S., III, 46) is as Romantic as you can get. Much of the essay is transparently tendentious. A major portion of it is devoted to a historical survey of the arts of dance, music, and poetry, full of inaccuracies and misinterpretations, and fanatically tailored to the argument for the future work of art. His portrayal of Beethoven's symphonies as a gradual approach to the basis of the *Gesamtkunstwerk* is a triumph of uninhibited tendentiousness. In Wagner's eyes, all history will culminate in his new form. This is "progressive Universalpoesie" with a vengeance. Wagner stubbornly insists that the separate arts, music alone, poetry alone, dance alone, are sterile. Since the dissolution of the *Gesamtkunstwerk* of the Greek drama, each has developed separately, but the whole long history of poetry, music, and the dance is one continuous picture of the separate phases of art, incomplete in themselves, attempting by various subterfuges to make up for their own deficiencies. Poets, composers, and choreographers invented substitutes for the needed synthesis or attempted in various feeble ways to develop within the separate arts the capabilities belonging to those other phases with which they were no longer associated.

Beethoven's creative act of synthesis, which paved the way for the (Wagnerian) art-work of the future, was, according to Wagner, an intuitive one. From the period when Beethoven no longer was content to write "pretty" music, but ever more strongly felt the urge to express himself more concretely and exactly, the nature of his music is radically altered. Wagner hears in the later works the ever more insistent desire for a precision of expression of which music is incapable. Beethoven's art culminates in the triumphant solution in the final movement of the *Ninth*, with its musical-poetic synthesis. The only possible creative step beyond this is the art-work of the future.

The positive content of *The Art-Work of the Future* is the clear exposition of the esthetic basis of a synthesis of the arts. In this work, Wagner leaves even *Lohengrin* far behind and envisions an art form which manifests a genuine, continuous, and thorough union of the separate arts. This synthesis is in a real sense a culmination, for it is an expression, not only of the romantic drive for a union of the arts as we encounter it in the theories and experiments of Tieck, Novalis, Schelling, Hoffmann, and others. It channels into this stream the eighteenth-century doctrine of the limitation of the arts, for Wagner is in his own way as firm about the boundaries surrounding poetry, visual movement, and music as Lessing was in his *Laocoön*. Indeed, *The Art-Work of the Future* is in some ways the answer to the tentative suggestions toward a synthesis made by Lessing in the sketches for a Part II of *Laocoön*.

The spectator, Wagner argues, both sees and hears the performer. With his eye he perceives not only the external figure and its movements as they are conditioned by its physical surroundings, but also the emotional and intellectual inner being through the facial expression and involuntary gestures, the impulse for which comes from within.

The ear of the spectator perceives simultaneously the tone of voice and the details of the speech of the actor. Through the tone of his voice (or by extension, in vocal musical expression without reference to the words used), the actor registers his feelings—of joy or pain, for example—most powerfully and most directly, thus supplementing the visual communication. But this direct communication, either alone or in conjunction with the visual perception, finds its limitation at the point where more precision of communication is needed. This is the province of speech, with its almost unlimited ability to articulate by selective description, simile, comparison, etc. In giving up its sense of pleasure in the sensuous element of its own expression, language acquires a precision of which the other elements of the synthesis are incapable.

Yet conversely, speech finds its limitations at those great moments where the individual feeling has reached a point where the particular, the arbitrary, gives way to the general and involuntary, "where the individual escapes out of the egoism of his limited personal feeling into the universal realm of great all-encompassing emotion." (W.S., III, 65) Here he must enlist the aid of the sensual tone of voice, the gesture of the body, and the expression of the face; "for where it is a question of the most direct and yet surest expression of the most exalted, the truest of which human expression is capable, man in his entirety must be in evidence, and this whole man is intellectual man united with physical and emotional man, not any one of these by itself." (W.S., III, 66) "Thus the united sister arts will appear, now all together, now in pairs, and again singly, according to the need of the dramatic action, which is the sole criterion. Now plastic mimicry will listen to the passionless weighing of thought; now resolute thought will pour itself into the expressive mold of gesture; now tone will express alone the outpouring of emotion; but again all three united will raise the will of the drama to direct and potent deed." (W.S., III, 157)

Wagner alludes to the function of the orchestra only briefly in this essay. His reference is reminiscent of the definition constructed ten years previously in A Pilgrimage to Beethoven, where he defined the instruments as the primal organs of nature, whose function was to surround the more expressive vocal organ with primitive emotion in its most universal sense. In the present essay, he conceives the orchestra as the harmonic means for supporting the individual with a foundation of universal emotion from which the personalized feeling of the actor can differentiate itself. (W.S., III, 157) The orchestra is to dissolve the static immovable basis of the actual scene into a fluent ethereal surface, whose basis is pure emotion.

Such is the theory of the ideal drama as set forth in *The Art-Work of the Future*. In its assumption that a more comprehensive massing together of effects will produce a more sublime artistic effect, it is typically Romantic. It is, of course, subject to Schopenhauer's objection that "grand opera is the creation not of a pure artistic sense but of the somewhat barbaric notion that esthetic enjoyment can be heightened by amassing the means, by the simultaneity of totally distinct varieties of impression, and that the effect can be strengthened by an increase in the total mass." (A.S., V, 457) But it is a logical stage in the direction Wagner had been travelling ever since *The Flying Dutchman*. He sees his art-work of the future as a kind of modern equivalent of the Greek drama, as indeed Nietzsche was later to argue.

Wagner will expand and elaborate this plan for a synthesis of the arts in the following *Opera and Drama*, but with one significant shift in emphasis. The role of the spoken word is prominent in the theory of *The Art-Work of the Future*. Wagner's outline would seem to require the use of spoken dialog at times during the drama. This is an indication of its proximity to the stage in his career where spoken drama seemed the likely solution. No completed stage work of Wagner's, however, permits the conceptual alone as embodied in the words of the dialog to assume so dominant a role as he provides for it in *The Art-Work of the Future*. Indeed, that Wagner recognized this discrepancy after finishing the essay is indicated by a footnote which he presumably added as an afterthought, in which he attempts to forestall any such interpretation. At those times, he says, when dramatic speech should dominate, the music is to subordinate itself to this speech completely. "But music possesses the ability of molding itself so imperceptibly to the thoughtful element of language that it can leave the latter in full control while acting as a support to it. . . . Thoughts and situations in which even the most gentle and reserved support of music would seem intrusive and burdensome would simply have no place

in the art-work of the future." (W.S., III, 160) Thus Wagner provides for continuous musical accompaniment throughout the
drama but in a manner which clearly implies a predominance of
the element of speech over music which can be found nowhere in
his works.

chapter eight
Opera and Drama

CONSIDERED as Wagner originally intended it, as a
theoretical counterpart of the *Ring* dramas which were maturing
within him even as he was constructing a pattern for them, *The
Art-Work of the Future* was inadequate. It was too general to be of
any practical use as a guide to fashioning a new art form (this is
particularly true in regard to the function of the orchestra), and
it still did not spell out clearly enough to suit Wagner the manner
of the organic synthesis of poetic verse and vocal melody which was
the nucleus of the entire theory. This need for a more detailed and
practical formula for the complex interrelationships he was about
to attempt became so clear to him that he was willing, even though
he had already spent precious months in theorizing, to take out
still another full year in order to expand and perfect the theory.

It is above all the amazing blueprint for the *Gesamtkunstwerk*
in Part III of *Opera and Drama* which makes this work of far
greater importance for us than its predecessor. We have every right
to use it in detail as a frame of reference when considering *The
Rhinegold, The Valkyrie,* and the first two acts of *Siegfried,* which
were the first works to come from his pen after he was finished with
his theory. The application to the later works must be made with
much greater caution than has been exercised hitherto, for reasons
to be thoroughly discussed later. This parallelism between the
theory and the early parts of the *Ring* is the result of the fact that
it had become clear to Wagner in the course of the three years
since the completion of *Lohengrin* that the Nibelungen work was
to be his next artistic production, and it is this project which
guides his thinking as he elaborates the artistic synthesis in Part
III of *Opera and Drama.* In November 1848, before leaving

Dresden, Wagner had written a poetic text, *Siegfried's Death,*
which in a much revised form ultimately became *Twilight of the
Gods.* There is no doubt at all that the general configuration of
the poetic verse in *Siegfried's Death* influenced Wagner in his
arguments in *Opera and Drama.* On the other hand, these arguments carry Wagner a good deal beyond the text of that poem, so
that when it was revised into *Twilight of the Gods,* it was ex-
tensively altered along the lines of the theory. Here we have a
striking instance of the reciprocal influence of theory and practice.
No music had been written and hence it is impossible to know
precisely to what extent Wagner as an artist had conceived the
interrelationships of the text, stage picture, and music which he
elucidated in such amazing detail in *Opera and Drama,* but it is
certain that his creative instinct was guiding him in this part of
the theory as well. "Let me say that even the boldest strokes of the
dramatic-musical form which I was postulating came to me because
I had in mind at the same time the plan for my great Nibelungen
drama, of which I had already written one part [the text of *Siegfried's Death*]. At this time, the conception was maturing in a way
that made my theory little more than an abstract expression of the
productive artistic process which was taking shape within me,"
wrote Wagner later in "Music of the Future." (W.S., VII, 118)

   The Art-Work of the Future had originally appeared with a dedication to Ludwig Feuerbach, whom Wagner at this period greatly
admired. Though the dedication was later removed, the philosopher's influence on the style and ideas in it and *Opera and Drama*
are evident on every page. Wagner's *Gesamtkunstwerk* in *Opera
and Drama* is ideologically a mixture of Feuerbach's materialistic
sensationalism and Romantic emotionalism; it is predicated on the
assumption that it can communicate only to the senses and through
them exclusively to the emotions. Reason, the conceptual and intellectual, are to play no part. "The combining intellect must have
nothing to do with the dramatic work of art. In the drama we must
become knowers through feeling. . . . This feeling, however, becomes intelligible to itself only through itself; it understands no
other language but its own. Things which can be explained only
by the infinite accommodations of the intellect are incomprehensi-
ble and disturbing to the feeling." (W.S., IV, 78) The long pre-

history of this idea, which according to Oscar Walzel is related to the drive of the Romantic artist to eliminate all traces of conscious intellectual activity from the work of art, is discussed at some length in his book, *Richard Wagner in seiner Zeit und nach seiner Zeit.*

This premise made possible the adjustment of the relative importance of the poem and the music which we have seen was needed in *The Art-Work of the Future.* For it brought with it automatically a significant increase in the importance of music, the language of emotions par excellence. But now the necessity presented itself of integrating the poetic dialog, conceptual speech, into the structure of a dramatic work whose sole appeal is to the emotions. Drawing in part on the experience he had gained in writing *Siegfried's Death,* but going far beyond that work in his exposition, he devises an ingenious way of emotionalizing the intellectual content of the poetry by the intensification of the direct sensory appeal of the verse. The artistic counterpart of this plan is to be found in the verse patterns of the *Ring* (and, to a lesser extent, in the later works), which have been such a happy hunting ground for those who wish to disparage Wagner. And indeed, it must be admitted that his verse sometimes borders on the ludicrous. However, as Wagner's artistic instinct must have told him, it proves in many respects to be a remarkably effective component of his word-tone synthesis, and deserves more sympathetic attention than it ordinarily receives, especially from those who judge it from the printed page.

The three most prominent characteristic features of his theoretical verse form are alliteration, condensation, and free rhythm. Alliteration, Wagner contends, can—and in more primitive times did—express an intuitive perception of the relationship between different objects or qualities (as in "Lust" and "Leid"). Condensation of the language permits a higher percentage of root syllables, which, according to Wagner's (and the Romantic) theory, derive from the early, intuitive stages of language development. It also eliminates to a large extent elements such as conjunctions and prepositions, which bear no emotional quality. Free rhythm replaces the regular rhythmic pulsation of most poetry with normal speech rhythm, thus making possible an endless degree of subtlety in accentuation for purposes of emotional shading. We will see in later chapters how these principles are carried out in the verse of his subsequent works.

In a dubious attempt to give this kind of poetry an impressive pedigree, Wagner delved into the problem of the origin of language, using in general Herder's point of departure (as in his *Origin of Language*), to the effect that language originated in the need felt by the human to express his emotional reactions to his surroundings by the utterance of sound. Vowel sounds, without consonants, Wagner writes, were the most primitive utterances of man, the involuntary expression of inner feeling. (W.S., IV, 92f.) Later, he contends, consonants were added to express more concisely the emotional reactions stimulated by the different objects than was possible with the vowel sound alone. Primitive man eventually progressed to the instinctive use of alliterative consonants to express various relationships among objects, or his reactions to these objects. The basis of this speech was strongly melodic, because the root vowels, which are the basis of musical tone, were still prominent. Much later, when the natural relationship of man to his surroundings gave way to a more artificial association, based on arbitrary laws of convention and custom, with a consequent submergence of involuntary emotion in favor of reflective intellectual activity, speech lost its melody, alliteration broke down, and prose was the result. From then on, speech was primarily a matter for intellect. The language of today is the means by which intellect addresses intellect, and as such cannot be used in the ideal drama.

But if the art-work of the future cannot use the ordinary language of today, neither can it use modern poetic verse, because of its artificial rhythmic patterns, which are foreign to the genius of the language, and rhyme, which throws into relief, not the essential part of the phrase, but the last word in the line. (W.S., IV, 103f.) Even the existence of Shakespeare and Goethe cannot prevent Wagner in the heat of his argument from heaping coals of scorn on iambic verse. He calls lines of iambic pentameter "five-footed monsters," and adds, "the ugliness of this meter as it appears in our dramas is purely and simply an offense to our feelings." (W.S., IV, 106) Music set to such poetry, by its stronger rhythmic quality, either accentuates the underlying rhythm, thereby heightening its inherent artificiality, or disregards it altogether, forcing its own more natural rhythm upon the poetic verse and dominating the words to the point where they become unintelligible. (W.S., IV, 112f.)

When one reflects that Wagner is attempting to claim that the kind of verse he was soon to write for the *Ring* dramas was a return to the language of a Golden Age before it was spoiled by the sophisticated overlay of a more complex civilization, the full ludicrousness of the argument becomes evident. Here is yet another instance where Wagner's pretensions are too extravagant. But for the purposes of a clear understanding of the *Gesamtkunstwerk,* all this is irrelevant. We need to take the verse as it exists, and examine it as to its suitability for a word-tone synthesis, and when we do this we will see that there is much to be said for it.

It is when Wagner launches upon the task of uniting this theoretical verse with vocal melody that he produces the most amazing discussion of musical prosody that has ever been written. Even if we were to discount the rest of Wagner's theory as purely personal rationalization with no general validity, and make no claim that it offers any original contribution to art theory or to philosophical thought, this synthesis of word and music must be acknowledged as an epochal contribution.

For his *Gesamtkunstwerk* Wagner needed an organic union of melodic line with poetic verse far more vital than the mere setting of a poetic text to music. He demanded a melodic configuration at every point so intimately fused with the poetic verse that the melody would be felt as the actual musical counterpart of that text; or better, as the musical portion of an indivisible unit, which he called "die Versmelodie" ("melodic verse"). By this fusion, the vocal line, drawing on the immense resources of music, would complete the emotionalization of the poetic line demanded by his original premise of an exclusive appeal to emotion.

This union of word and tone is the very core of the synthesis propounded in *Opera and Drama.* Wagner asserts that when the precise quantitative relation between accented and unaccented syllables of the poetic verse is observed by the melodic line, the stronger rhythmic force of the music will strengthen the basic pattern of the verse, making possible the articulation of emotional subtleties otherwise impossible to record. For by means of the melodic line, the unaccented syllables as well as the secondary accents can be placed in a dynamic relationship and can sweep up to a climax or fall away from it, as the sense requires. Various devices are at the disposal of the poet-composer for expressing even the most minute variations. He can place the accented or unaccented syllables on stronger or weaker portions of his musical measure. In a measure with four beats, for example, ordinarily the first is the strongest, the third has a secondary accent, the second is unaccented, and the fourth is the weakest of all. Other types of measure have different combinations of accents. He can set the words to more or less emphatic steps on the tonal scale. The tonic, supertonic, mediant, etc. (the *do, re, mi* relationships) possess definite gradations of importance in their relations as steps of the scale. He can also fix them on a higher or lower pitch. Wagner describes most minutely the procedure for the construction of these divisions. The following he gives as an example: "Let us assume an expression which contains three accents in one breath, of which the first is the strongest, the second (as is usually the case) the weakest, and the third again stronger. The poet would then as a matter of course arrange a phrase of two measures, of which the first would have the strongest accent in its 'good' half, the weakest in its 'bad' half, and the second measure would have the third accent on its down beat. The 'bad' half of the second measure would serve for taking breath and as an upbeat to the first measure of the second rhythmic phrase, which would need to be an appropriate repetition of the first. In such a phrase, the unaccented portions would mount as an upbeat to the accent of the first measure, would descend from this to its 'bad' half, and from here rise again as an up beat to the 'good' half of the second measure. The strengthening of the second accent which might perhaps be called for by the sense of the phrase would be easily effected rhythmically (as well as by raising the pitch of the melody) by allowing either the unaccented portion between it and the first accent, or by allowing the up beat to the third to be omitted entirely. This would draw increased attention to such an intermediate accent." (W.S., IV, 125) The possibilities for variation of such patterns are limitless.

A rhythmic phrase, or breath group, fashioned in this way, forms a small unit, to which must be added another phrase rhythmically and melodically complementary to it, and conditioned by the contour of the first. For the second must be so conceived that it constitutes a strengthening or quieting repetition of the first. This is necessary because "a melody can impress itself forcefully on the hearing only if it contains a repetition of certain melodic elements in a certain rhythm. If such do not recur, the melody lacks the very unifying bond which makes it a melody in the first place." (W.S., IV, 114)

It is at moments of emotional stress when the poetic-melodic synthesis attains an unprecedented expressive ability. At such moments, when the spoken word alone is used, the speaker involuntarily expresses the increased tension or emotional excitement by stressing the sensuous quality of the words he is speaking, particularly of the key syllables. But he can do this only to a certain point, beyond which the speech becomes sing-song or drawling. (W.S., IV, 124) In the melodic verse of the ideal drama, says Wagner, the emotional content, especially of the climactic moments, can be realized to the fullest, because the key syllable of the poetic line is identical with the climactic tone of the melodic line. The "tönender Laut" ("sounding vowel") is transformed into a "lautender Ton" ("sounding tone") (W.S., IV, 135), which can be indefinitely prolonged. This extension of the vowel sound can be so regulated as to express parallel or contrasting relationships with other extended vowel sounds from other poetic-musical phrases. Thus a kind of vowel alliteration, impossible in spoken verse, is achieved.

But the potentialities of music for expression of emotional interrelationships between elements of the musical-poetic line are greatest in its extension of consonantal alliteration. In poetry, alliterative cross relationships are possible only between consonants which are phonetically similar and in close proximity. (W.S., IV, 140) But in the musical-poetic verse, by means of key relationships expressed through modulation from one key to another, a more extensive alliteration is possible. Here, too, a variety of techniques is available to the poet-composer. Large sections involving eight or ten or more lines of poetry can be drawn together by successive modulations into more and more distant keys until the furthest point is reached, when the modulatory progression can return by degrees to the original key. At the other extreme, sudden, unprepared modulations can be used to underline unexpected deviations in the poetic line. Employing the only concrete illustration used in this entire essay, Wagner constructs the poetic lines, "Die Liebe bringt Lust und Leid, / doch in ihr Weh auch webt sie Wonnen" ("Love brings delight and sorrow, / but into her woe she weaves delights"). (W.S., IV, 152f.) On the word "Leid," he explains, the music would modulate into a contrasting, but related, key and remain in that key until the end of the second line, where a transitional modulation back to the original key would take place on the word "webt," thus linking "Wonnen" with "Lust," and "Leid" with "Weh" as parallel; while "Lust" and "Leid," as well as "Weh" and "Wonnen," would be linked as contrasting. There are some amazing examples of this technique in the Wagnerian drama.

The orchestra is needed, of course, to realize the modulation embodied in the melodic verse, since modulation is basically harmonic in character. The harmonic and instrumental resources of the orchestra in general are to be employed at all times by the poet-composer as a further means of underlining the emotional content of the melodic verse. (W.S., IV, 167f.) Wagner claims in *Opera and Drama* that the absolute musician has hesitated to fathom harmonic depths because he has had no compelling purpose to justify their use. (W.S., IV, 149) Twenty-eight years later, in 1879, he elaborates this statement into an essay "On the Application of Music to the Drama." (W.S., X, 176–93)

The most creative function of the orchestra envisioned by Wagner in this remarkable blueprint for the *Gesamtkunstwerk* is what he calls presentiments and reminiscences. It is quite clear to see that Wagner thought of these as complementary and equally important functions of the orchestra, yet it is equally plain that the reminiscences could be much more precisely defined and that they were a far more effective integrating device. The motifs of reminiscence are the theoretical prototypes of what are now universally termed "leitmotifs," a term which was never used by

Wagner but was coined later by Hans von Wolzogen, who wrote the first guides to the musical motifs in Wagner's dramas.

However, a sharp distinction of fundamental importance must be drawn between the theoretical motif of reminiscence and the leitmotifs as they appear in Wagner's dramas. The very specific requirements of the theoretical motifs are fulfilled even partially by only a small percentage of the actual musical leitmotifs. That is to say, Wagner in his practice departed almost at once from his theory in this respect. For example, about half of the motifs in *The Rhinegold* resemble the theory closely enough to be considered genuine motifs of reminiscence. *The Valkyrie* and *Siegfried* show a rapid departure from this technique. With *Tristan and Isolde* the phenomenon of leitmotif no longer bears much resemblance to the theoretical model.

At moments of extremest excitement or most complete repose, where the momentary situation is not conditioned by any reminiscence of something past, the musical-poetic verse contains nothing which cannot be revealed fully by its own expression, supplemented by gesture and orchestra harmony and tone color. But there often occur moments when the immediate expression is influenced by the thought of something lying in the past which continues to have an emotional effect on the speaker. The presence and consequently the influence of this reminiscence can be communicated by the repetition of the characteristic melodic line which was part of the original expression. The melodic line alone, originally the musical counterpart of the idea contained in the verse, is sufficient to inject this idea as a conditioning element of reminiscence into the new situation. It thus appears as the realization and representation of what was just thought of by the character on the stage. (W.S., IV, 184) Even when such a reminiscence occurs against the will of the character, the fact of its having conditioned his present reaction can be communicated in this way.

Wagner's discussion of these motifs of reminiscence is at times involved and obscure. Although he is not clear about it, there is some reason for thinking that he intended the characteristic melodic line containing the reminiscence to be used in its first repetition as the melodic line of the verse conditioned by this reminiscence. Under such circumstances, it would need to be altered to adjust to the new words but still retain a contour which was at once identifiable by the audience. In such an instance, it would function as the melodic counterpart of the thought revealed by the poetic verse. After this first repetition, which would establish it as a motif of reminiscence, it could become the property of the orchestra. Wagner assumed that the motif, repeated either in the melodic line or by the orchestra, would be immediately associated by the listener with the verse with which it originally occurred, and the necessary relationship between past and present automatically established. If he did mean to add this further requirement as a fixed part of the motif of reminiscence, even fewer examples of the device in its purest form are to be found in the works to follow.

These reminiscences are to be called into play, according to *Opera and Drama,* during the moments when the poetic level of the melodic verse must fall off in the interest of more clearly defining the dramatic situation. (W.S., IV, 199f.) Their use is to be entirely functional. Wagner cautions that they are for the purpose of elucidation and are not to be used merely to bolster the interest where the dramatic situation has allowed it to lag. A single motif used without proper justification is sufficient to destroy the unity. They are to recede into the background when the emotional level of the melodic verse again rises.

Wagner leaves no room for doubt that the poetic-musical verse is to be the source of his motifs of reminiscence. Being thus derived from a specific thought expressed by a specific individual in a specific situation, they acquire an exactness which is not the property of orchestral motifs (or of many of the motifs Wagner himself later constructs in disregard of this theoretical position). "Music cannot think," says Wagner, "but it can materialize thoughts; that is, it can make known their emotional contents as no longer merely recollected but made present." It can do this, though, only if it is a musical motif which is conditioned by the poetic verse. Then and only then does its repetition communicate a definite emotion, "the emotion of one who at the moment feels the need to express a new feeling which derives from the first—now no longer expressed by him, but made perceptible to our senses by the orchestra." (W.S., IV, 185) The sounding of this motif unites a non-present conditioning emotion with the present one conditioned by it.

The genuine motifs of reminiscence, then, are a powerful device for binding together and tightening the structure of the musical drama and represent something far more vital and dynamic than the tag system devised by the many guides to the musical motifs in Wagner's works.

The presentiments, thought of by Wagner as a kind of counterpart of the reminiscences, are a quite different matter. Here, although Wagner attempted to define their nature in the same practical terms, he was dealing with a much vaguer concept. He conceived of these motifs of presentiment as a kind of psychological and emotional preparation of the listener for what was to come, so that the situation, when it finally arrived, would be received as a fulfillment of the presentiment earlier awakened in his consciousness. "At those moments when there is no gesture, and melodic speech is silent, when the drama is preparing its future course in inner moods as yet unuttered, these still unspoken moods can be expressed by the orchestra in such a manner that their manifestation acquires the character of a presentiment conditioned by the poet's aim." (W.S., IV, 186)

Thus the presentiment is conceived as the reflection of a feeling which is real enough but which has not yet been placed in connection with a specific object. Wagner uses the simile of a harp which stands ready to be played, whose strings are vibrated by the passing wind. Since it necessarily precedes the situation or object to which it refers, however, it cannot be derived from a definite poetic-musical situation, and is necessarily orchestral in origin. The most obvious examples of this technique are the preludes to the *Ring* dramas, but these are by no means the only ones, as we shall see. We shall further see that the necessary indefiniteness of this technique gives rise to a certain vagueness which makes the presentiments a source of the very ambiguities Wagner was at such pains to eliminate from his ideal drama.

It will be remembered that in *The Art-Work of the Future* Wagner did not elaborate on the function or functions of the orchestra in the work of synthesis. The coordination of gesture with the orchestra was not mentioned in the earlier essay, although it was implied. This coordination Wagner explicitly elaborates in *Opera and Drama*. The orchestra is to extend into the aural realm the emotional effect that gesture communicates in the visual. In this function, it is necessarily independent of the poetic-musical verse, since gesture and facial expression communicate with an immediacy and directness of which words are incapable. Yet precision is possible for the orchestra in such instances by virtue of the simultaneous visual-aural communication which excludes any possible ambiguity.

Perhaps the most sweeping innovation in Wagner's theoretical synthesis is his position with regard to ensemble singing. It will be remembered that in *Lohengrin* he had managed a remarkable degree of maneuverability and expressiveness in the choral parts, imparting to the choral mass a fluidity which one does not find elsewhere. Yet the theoretical framework of *Opera and Drama*, with its consistent drive toward precision and exactness, eliminates choral singing entirely; indeed, even ensemble singing, such as duets, trios, etc. is excluded. For, Wagner argues, the role of the chorus is assumed in a greatly more expressive manner by the orchestra, and in the art-work of the future there can appear no individual whose utterances are in any way to be considered as a harmonic or melodic support of another character.

In this last he hedges a little and parenthetically leaves the way open for ensemble singing at certain appropriate moments, but even here he is at pains to eliminate the traditional idea of duet, trio, etc. "Only in the full tide of lyric outpouring, when all the participants have been led to a joint expression of feeling, can the composer make use of the polyphonic mass of voices, to which he may transfer the manifestation of the harmony. But even here it will remain the task of the composer to make the character's share in the outpouring of feeling not mere harmonic support for the melody. In the harmonic texture, he must see to it that the individuality of the participants makes itself felt in definite melodic expression." (W.S., IV, 164) This is a large order, but we shall see that Wagner measures up to it, at least in the works produced by him immediately after the theory, *The Rhinegold*, *The Valkyrie*, and *Siegfried*, Acts I and II.

In considering the combination of all these novel elements, Wagner stresses the fundamental importance of the melodic verse. This is to be the basis of the entire dramatic structure, "the life-giving center of the dramatic expression." (W.S., IV, 190) The functions of the orchestra are at all times conditioned by it. The motifs of reminiscence are drawn directly from the contour of the melody of the melodic verse. The flow of harmony in the orchestra produces the modulation where called for in the melodic verse and at all times increases the emotional significance of what is being sung. Never must the orchestra indulge in harmonic or melodic devices not conditioned by the dramatic content. (W.S., IV, 199f.)

chapter nine

The Rhinegold

THE STYLISTIC gulf between *Lohengrin* and *The Rhinegold* is enormous. These two successive works differ more strikingly than any consecutive creations of any other composer or writer known to me. We have observed in the early works the gradual evolution of a new style in certain specific passages embodying the innovations, incorporated in structures which otherwise bore a noticeable resemblance to traditional opera. *The Rhinegold* is musically, poetically, and in every other way a clean break with tradition. The first work to be completed after *Opera and Drama*, it is the purest exemplification of that theory, for it is the only one which was finished before Wagner was subjected to additional influences modifying the force of that theory on his creative activity.

The chronology of the creation of the four *Ring* dramas is extremely involved. In its essentials, it is as follows: *Lohengrin* was finished in March 1848. In November of the same year, Wagner completed the poem of *Siegfried's Death,* which was later transformed into *Twilight of the Gods.* After this came the flight from Dresden and a three-year period of theoretical activity which yielded *The Art-Work of the Future* and *Opera and Drama.* The latter was finished early in 1851, and by June of that year the poem of *Young Siegfried* (now *Siegfried*) was completed. The poem of *The Valkyrie* followed in July 1852; *The Rhinegold* in November; and the thorough revision of *Siegfried's Death* into *Twilight of the Gods* in December 1852. Thus, the poems of the four dramas, substantially as we now have them, were composed in the following sequence: *Siegfried, The Valkyrie, The Rhinegold, Twilight of the Gods,* and all were finished before the music for any of them was begun.

The music was composed in normal sequence: *The Rhinegold* first, by May 1854; *The Valkyrie* by April 1856; and *Siegfried*, Acts I and II, in July 1857. There followed an interruption of twelve years. Act III of *Siegfried* was not begun until March 1869, and finished in February 1871. The final touches were put on *Twilight of the Gods* (and thus on the entire monumental work) in November 1874, twenty-six years after the first words were written.

The verse form of *The Rhinegold* is a faithful counterpart of the principles set forth in *Opera and Drama*. It is highly alliterative, compact, with root syllables predominating, and with irregular rhythm, as illustrated by the following excerpt from the closing scene:

> Abendlich strahlt der Sonne Auge;
> in prächtiger Glut prangt glänzend die Burg.
> In des Morgens Scheine mutig erschimmernd
> lag sie herrenlos, hehr verlockend vor mir.
> Von Morgen bis Abend, in Müh' und Angst,
> nicht wonnig ward sie gewonnen!
> Es naht die Nacht:
> vor ihrem Neid biete sie Bergung nun.
>
> (*Rheingold*, 210)

> (In the dusk the sun's eye beams;
> in a splendid glow shines gleaming the fortress.
> In morning light boldly shimmering
> it stood masterless, sublimely alluring before me.
> From morning to evening, in labor and anxiety,
> not blissfully was it won!
> The night approaches:
> from night's envy may it give refuge now.)

The lines are given as they are divided by the vocal line, not as they appear when printed as a poem without the music.

For special effects, Wagner employs more daring techniques, such as this partially comic alliteration when lecherous Alberich stumbles all over himself trying to reach one of the Rhine maidens in Scene 1:

> Garstig glatter glitsch'riger Glimmer! Wie gleit' ich aus!
>
> (*Rheingold*, 12)
>
> (Nasty smooth slippery rocks! How I slip!)

or this impressive concentrated language, expressive of the brute power and primitive thought processes of the giants Fasolt and Fafner:

Lichtsohn du, leicht gefügter! hör' und hüte dich; Verträgen halte
    Treu'!   (Rheingold, 71)

(Son of Light you, lightly formed! hear and beware: compacts keep
    loyally!)

In constructing the poetic-musical synthesis, Wagner subordinates the melodic element in *The Rhinegold* to the poetic verse more fully than he does in any other of the *Ring* dramas. This is a consistent development. For in the theory of this period we saw an original emphasis on the words (*The Art-Work of the Future*) and then an increase in the relative importance of music (*Opera and Drama*). The same phenomenon is to be observed in the dramas. *Lohengrin* was the culmination in the earlier works of the tendency to subordinate tone to word. *The Rhinegold* is the starting point for the trend in the opposite direction. There is nothing in *Opera and Drama* which fixes the exact degree of balance between word and tone in the melodic verse. The technique and the aims of the synthesis were clearly formulated, but the actual proportions remained to be worked out in the dramas themselves. As in *Lohengrin*, Wagner was often too careful in *The Rhinegold* to assimilate and subordinate the vocal melody to the poetic verse. Frequently this prevents the music from carrying out its function in the musical-poetic synthesis. The following typical example will illustrate this:

Fast schäm' ich mich   mit ih-nen zu schaf-fen;   zur
(*I am almost ashamed to associate with them;*   *to*

lek - ken-den Lo -   he   mich wie - der zu wan - deln,
a leaping flame to transform myself I feel an impelling

spür' ich lok - ken-de Lust: sie auf - zu-zeh-ren, die einst mich ge ·
desire: to consume those who once tamed me, instead of

zähmt, statt mit den Blin-den blöd zu ver-geh'n, und wä-ren es
foolishly perishing with the blind ones, though they were

gött - lich - ste Göt - ter!
the most godlike of gods!)

The melodic rhythm, the pitch, and accents are all carefully calculated to fit the poetic pattern. But the melody itself has not sufficient importance to be the emotional interpreter of the words in accordance with which it has been fashioned. The words themselves are the more effective portion of the combination. The music has very little intrinsic value.

What is needed to realize the aims of musical-poetic synthesis expressed in the theory is a musical line which will mold itself as carefully to the poetic verse as the melody in the above example, but which at the same time makes a significant contribution to the total effect. Only then can the melodic line be considered the musical counterpart of the words. There are times in *The Rhinegold* when this happens, and when it does, a genuine word-tone synthesis in the sense of *Opera and Drama* is produced. The following is the beginning of Alberich's curse, from Scene 4, and is the most impressive dramatic climax of the work:

(wütend lachend)
(laughing in a rage)

Bin ich nun frei?   wirk - lich frei?   so
(Am I now free?   *really free?*   *Then*

grüss' euch denn   mei-ner Frei - heit   er - ster Gruss!
let my freedom's first greeting   *greet you!*

Wie durch Fluch er mir ge - riet,   ver - flucht sei die - ser Ring!
As by a curse it came into my power, cursed be this ring!)

The melody fits the declamatory rhythm perfectly. The spasmodic character of the two short introductory phrases is heightened by the pauses. The bitter sarcasm of "wirklich" is intensified by the exaggerated jump in pitch. The ominous quality of the succeeding verse is effected by the monotony of pitch and is a forceful transition into the curse itself, which rises with an irresistible drive to a fortissimo on "verflucht," where the climax, musically, poetically, and dramatically, is reached. Prolongation of the vowels, especially the three successive stages, "Fluch," "geriet," and "verflucht," plays its essential part in extending and intensifying the climactic moment. The melodic contour, especially of the curse itself, sweeps the attention onward to the climax, making use of each unaccented note to further the progress toward the top accent in a manner which would be impossible without the melodic line. The orchestra, too, is ingeniously brought into play. The first eight measures are supported by the first appearance of a sinister syncopated theme, associated with Alberich's hatred and his work of destruction throughout the entire *Ring*. The curse itself is accompanied only by F♯ tympani, which begin softly and crescendo with the melodic line to a fortissimo on the climax.

This is an excellent example of the word-tone synthesis of *Opera and Drama*. Everything depends on the sense of the words. The musical line would make little sense, except in so far as it interprets emotionally the content of the verse. But, as that interpreter, it possesses great emotional power. It does not force the verse into any unnaturalness, it does not attract the attention away from the verse. Word and tone, each contributing its share to the synthesis, are blended inseparably into a single unit which combines utmost precision with a wide emotional range.

The force of Wagner's synthesis is best illustrated in such climactic moments. But it is not limited to them. It can be effective also where the emotional level is less intense. The following is an extract from Loge's long narrative in Scene 2:

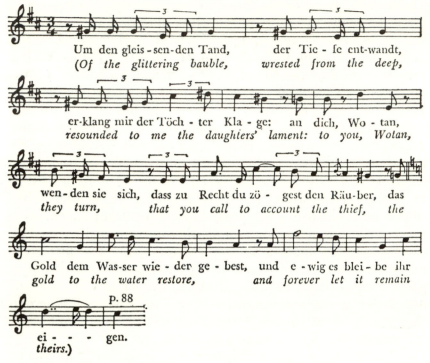

Um den gleis - sen-den Tand,   der Tie - fe ent-wandt,
(Of the glittering bauble,   wrested from the deep,

er-klang mir der Töch - ter Kla - ge: an dich, Wo - tan,
resounded to me the daughters' lament: to you, Wotan,

wen-den sie sich,   dass zu Recht du zö - gest den Räu-ber, das
they turn,   that you call to account the thief,   the

Gold dem Was-ser wie - der ge - best, und e - wig es blei - be ihr
gold to the water restore,   and forever let it remain

p. 88

ei - - - gen.
theirs.)

The orchestra is an essential part of this word-tone amalgamation. "Den gleissenden Tand" of the first measure refers to the Rhinegold, which has been stolen by Alberich. The first eight measures are accompanied by a minor variation of the Rhinegold theme, which was first heard, in bright major harmonies, in Scene 1, where it was sung by the Rhine maidens in praise of the gold they were guarding. Their lament over its loss is expressed here by the minor variation. The melodic line of the first two measures is based on the Nibelung theme (which appears in its complete form some pages later) and links the theft with the Nibelungs. The melodic line of the third and fourth measures is based on a minor variation of the second part of the Rhinegold theme and is designed to express the "Klage." The following "an dich, Wotan, wenden sie sich" is set with special care for the liveliness of the declamatory rhythm and accent, because it is direct address. With the implication that Wotan will come to their aid and restore the gold to the rightful owners, the Rhinegold theme appears in the accompaniment in its original major form from then on to the end of the example. The melodic line, from here to the end, is based on the major harmonies of the accompanying Rhinegold theme, and there is an ever broader sweep to the line as it progresses, with a final C major flourish on "ewig es bleibe ihr eigen."

This kind of intimate fusion of poetic and melodic line makes possible in lyric drama a rich character delineation in detail such as had been impossible before this time. There is nothing in opera preceding Wagner, or indeed even in Wagnerian opera itself before *Opera and Drama,* that approaches the subtlety, the fullness, the exactness of character portrayal that is now possible through Wagner's invention of this kind of dialog. The sinister force of Alberich, Mime's bungling stupidity, Loge's slyness, and the characterizations of the other chief personages bring a new dimension to the lyric drama.

Musical pictorializations of individual words and phrases were first pointed out in the chapter on *Tannhäuser* (see pp. 47–48). In *Lohengrin,* Wagner's attempt to capture the speech rhythm (see p. 51) precluded such special musical effects. Now, in *The Rhinegold,* whose concentrated alliterative verse is very conducive to such a technique, musical pictorialization of individual words reappears, this time in profusion. However, since in *The Rhinegold* the word, in general, dominates tone, the musical descriptions are not as frankly and as boldly musical as they will become later on, in *The Valkyrie* for example, where the music assumes greater relative importance. The following are four examples of pictorializations from *The Rhinegold:*

Pfui!   du haa - ri - ger,   höck - ri - ge Geck!
(Fie!   you hairy hunchbacked fop!

Schwar - zes, schwie - li - ges Schwe - fel - ge - zwerg!
black, horny-skinned sulphurous dwarf!)

p. 17

Heh - ier— herr - li-cher Baul
(*Noble splendid structure!*)

schö - - nem · Schmuck?
(*beautiful adornment?*)

an .den   Ä - sten darbt und dorrt   das Obst, bald
(*on the branches withers and fades the fruit,   soon*)

fällt   faul   es her - ab,
it will rot and fall,)

In *Opera and Drama* Wagner specifically required that a given
unit of poetic verse and melody be followed by an answering unit
which resembled the first sufficiently to be considered complementary to it. The reason he gave for this was that "a melody can
impress itself forcefully on the hearing only if it contains a repetition of certain melodic elements in a certain rhythm. If such do
not recur, the melody lacks the very unifying bond which makes
it a melody in the first place." (W.S., IV, 114) There is a resemblance in this definition to the traditional technique of the answering phrase. However, the latter implies a melodic line which
is worked out for musical purposes only, the relationship to the
poetic verse being a secondary matter. Wagner's definition implies,
first of all, organic word-tone synthesis, constructed in such a manner that the "return" of definite melodic moments in a definite
rhythm corresponding to a similar parallel construction of the
verse is effected.

Careful examination of the score will reveal that the greatest
number of poetic-melodic units in *The Rhinegold* are followed
by complementary units. But the impression given by an actual

performance is just the opposite. The parallel construction is seldom noticed, the repetitions often seem to be missing. The chief reason for this is again the lack of emphasis on the melodic line in comparison to the poetic verse. It often is of such slight importance that it contains nothing to fasten the attention of the listener, and the force of the repetition is not felt. This can be clearly seen in the illustration on page 83. It is the chief defect of Wagner's melodic verse in *The Rhinegold* and is more pronounced there than in either *The Valkyrie* or *Siegfried,* where the melodic line is consistently of greater significance. Sometimes even in important speeches, the rhythmic or melodic repetition is actually lacking. In the example below, the poetic verses form a definite unit linked together from first to last by alliteration ("gleicht"—"Glücke"— "Gewinn"—"Gold"—"vergabst"; "viel"—"Feinde"—"fällen"— "vergabst"; "nun"—"genommen"—"nützt"), but the melodic line has almost no pattern at all:

Was gleicht, Wo - tan, wohl dei - nem Glük - ke?
(*What is like your good fortune, Wotan?*

Viel er-warb dir des Rin - ges Ge-winn; dass er
Much you gained by the winning of the ring; that it

nun dir ge - nom - men, nützt dir noch mehr:
has been taken from you benefits you even more:

dei-ne Fein - de sieh! fäl - len sich selbst um das
your enemies, see! slay each other over the

p. 201

Gold, das du ver - gabst.
gold that you gave away.)

On the other hand, when the melodic line does possess sufficient importance to impress itself upon the attention of the listener, the repetition has meaning, and the poetic-melodic synthesis Wagner was striving for is attained. The example on page 86 illustrates this clearly.

There is an enormous amount of alliteration in the poem of *The Rhinegold*. Much of it is simply a poetic device, however, and does not reveal "inner relationships" between the alliterated words, as Wagner insisted it should do in *Opera and Drama*. Nor is there anything approaching consistency in his musical treatment of alliteration. *The Rhinegold* contains no patterns which are as neatly constructed as the two lines, "Die Liebe bringt Lust und Leid,/doch in ihr Weh auch webt sie Wonnen," which he used as an illustration in his theory (see p. 74). The following unit comes as close to it as any:

> Nur Wonne schafft dir
> Was mich erschreckt?
> Dich freut die Burg,
> Mir bangt es um Freia.

The technique of *Opera and Drama* would require the music to highlight the alliterative relationship of the two contrasting pairs of lines. Actually, nothing is made of it:

In some instances, however, alliteration is used in conjunction with conceptual parallels and contrasts, and the music is then fashioned in a manner complementary to it. The feeling of parallel or contrast is thus intensified, extended, and carried further into the emotional sphere, and a sense of musical-poetic unity results which carries out Wagner's intentions in *Opera and Drama*. The following is from Scene 1:

Nur wer der Min - ne Macht ent - sagt, nur wer der
(Only he who love's power renounces, only he who

p. 43

Lie - be Lust ver - jagt,
love's delights banishes,)

A parallel in meaning would of course be perceived between
"Minne Macht" and "Liebe Lust" even if they were not alliterated. But the alliteration serves to focus the esthetic attention on
the parallel, and to add to its emotional effect. Thus, even without
the music, the relationship is pointedly expressed by the verse.
Now, with an exact repetition of the melodic contour, this feeling
of parallel is made more forceful by its extension into the more
highly emotional sphere of music. The dual expression is welded
into a firm single unit, and all the smaller poetic alliterative units
included within it are felt to be closely related. This is what
Wagner spoke of as musical alliteration.

A somewhat different example:

> Deiner Untreu' trau' ich, nicht deiner Treu'!
> Doch getrost trotz' ich euch Allen!

These two verses are spoken by Alberich in Scene 3. A contrast
between the two lines is here accentuated by the alliteration. But
the contrast is stressed, far more than could be done with the
verse alone, by the addition of the musical line, as follows:

Dei - ner Un - treu' trau' ich, nicht dei - ner Treu'!
(Your faithlessness I trust, not your loyalty!

p. 136

Doch ge - trost trotz' ich euch Al - len!
But confidently I defy you all!)

"Untreu' " is emphasized by the longer note values; "Treu' " by the skip of a minor sixth to C. A modulation from A minor to A major occurs on "getrost," with its major third (C♯) in contrast to the minor third (C♮) on "Treu'." This change from minor to major, plus the extension of the vowel on "getrost," achieves a vivid contrast between the two halves of the phrase.

There are about fourteen musical-poetic alliterative syntheses of this character in *The Rhinegold*. In addition, there are at least three which extend the same principle over a longer span. The following verses are musically alliterated into a compact musical-poetic whole of twenty-eight measures by an extension of the principles just illustrated:

> Trügt mich ein Nebel? neckt mich ein Traum?
> Wie bang und bleich verblüht ihr so bald!
> Euch erlischt der Wangen Licht;
> der Blick eures Auges verblitzt!—
> Frisch, mein Froh! noch ist's ja früh!
> Deiner Hand, Donner, entsinkt ja der Hammer.
> Was ist's mit Fricka? freut sie sich wenig
> ob Wotans grämlichem Grau,
> das schier zum Greisen ihn schafft?   (*Rheingold,* 103f.)

> (Does a mist deceive me? Does a dream mock me?
> How wan and pale you grow so rapidly!
> The light vanishes from your cheeks;
> the fire in your eyes dies out!—
> Quick, Froh! it is still early!
> From your hand, Donner, the hammer sinks.
> What's wrong with Fricka? Is she unhappy
> about Wotan's morose greyness,
> which almost makes an old man of him?)

The most extended example of this kind is Alberich's curse, which is a poetic-melodic unit involving fifty-six measures.

Still another kind of musical alliteration is to be found in *The Rhinegold,* linking together poetic lines widely separated from one another. Alberich is transformed three different times by the magic of the Tarnhelm. Each of the incantations he uses is linked with the others, not only by similarity of poetic structure, but also by the pointed repetition of the same melodic line and of the accompanying distinctive Tarnhelm motif. The three lines are:

Nacht und Nebel, niemand gleich! (Night and mist, like no-one!)
(*Rheingold*, 118)

Riesenwurm winde sich ringelnd! (Giant dragon writhe and twist!)
(*Rheingold*, 150)

Krumm und grau krieche Kröte! (Crooked and gray crawl, toad!)
(*Rheingold*, 153)

The harmonic elucidation of the melodic verse by the orchestra functions strictly according to the principles of *Opera and Drama*. There are times when the orchestra support is very meagre, but there is never such complexity of harmony in the accompaniment that it attracts the attention away from the melodic verse to which the orchestra is supposed to be subordinate.

In *Opera and Drama*, the motif of reminiscence was designed to be the chief device by which unity of word-tone expression was to be attained in the ideal drama. It was intended to link present with past, to make clear hidden relationships, to impress emotionally upon the listener the force of a thought or deed recalled. Such motifs, by definition, were to be derived from the melodic verse. The melodic line associated with the original word-tone statement was to reappear at later points, whenever the statement itself was to be called to mind.

Wagner's frequent disregard of this principle in *The Rhinegold* is the chief reason why the orchestra tends from the very beginning to assume a greater importance in the music dramas than was intended in *Opera and Drama*. When the leitmotif is derived originally from a word-tone combination, and takes its meaning from the word content of the melodic verse, then, each time it is repeated, it serves as a link between the orchestra music and the musical-poetic line, because it automatically calls to mind the words of which it was originally the melodic counterpart. On the other hand, when the motif arises from the orchestra, it is purely musical, and throws the balance in favor of orchestra music.

Wagner himself did not identify the motifs by name. If the provisions of *Opera and Drama* had been strictly adhered to, this would have been unnecessary, as the words of the melodic verse would have provided the identity, and a firm word-tone relationship would have been established in all cases. When the motif originates in the orchestra, especially when the intended connotation is in doubt, there is inevitably a less intimate relationship between the text and the music. Almost half the motifs which appear in *The Rhinegold,* and an even larger proportion in the works to follow, have no connection with the melodic verse at all.

A clear example of the genuine motif of reminiscence is the Curse motif. The melodic line which was originally united with the words "Wie durch Fluch er mir geriet, verflucht sei dieser Ring!" (see p. 84) is repeated by the orchestra at moments throughout all the *Ring* dramas whenever reference to this curse is made, especially when its effects are seen in the subsequent catastrophes of the plot. Thus, when the two giants quarrel over possession of the ring and Fasolt is slain by Fafner, the motif is announced solemnly by the brass. The original curse is forcefully injected into the emotional picture by the motif's appearance. The original scene, the original words even, are recalled.

Another motif derived clearly from the melodic verse is that of the Rhinegold, sung first by the Rhine maidens to the words "Rheingold! Rheingold!" in the first scene. It appears in this first drama fifteen times. The accompaniment to the example on page 86 is derived from variations of this motif.

The central motif of all four Nibelungen dramas is the Ring motif. It alone has an additional connection with the theoretical motif of reminiscence. We have seen that Wagner's intention may have been that a motif must first be repeated in a new musical-poetic phrase as a thought recalled, in order that it be firmly fixed as a specific reminiscence, before it could be taken up by the orchestra alone, somewhat as the "Verbot" theme was treated in *Lohengrin.* If he had really intended this additional feature, and there is some doubt about it because of the obscurity of Wagner's exposition in the essay, he disregarded it except in the one instance of the Ring motif. The first line of the example below is sung by a Rhine maiden; the second, sixty-two bars later, by Alberich:

Der Welt Er - be ge - wän-ne zu ei - gen, wer aus dem
(*The heritage of the world he would win who from*

p. 41

Rhein - gold schü - fe den Ring,
the Rhinegold created the ring,)

p. 47

Der Welt Er - be ge - wänn' ich zu ei - gen durch dich?
(*The heritage of the world I would win through you?)*

After these two appearances in the melodic verse, the motif becomes the property of the orchestra, appearing in *The Rhinegold*
alone fifty-one times.

Those motifs, approximately half of the total, which are not
derived from the melodic line, cannot be called motifs of reminiscence. They appear for the first time in the orchestra and are not
associated with any word-tone expression. The distinction is not
unessential. A motif, the Valhalla motif, for example, which appears only in the orchestra, and reappears when Valhalla is referred
to, does not link past with present. It does infuse the verse with a
more intense emotional aura but is not a motif of reminiscence
and has not the inseparable connection with word-tone synthesis
that actual examples of this technique possess. It is a musical
device, and, if at all elaborate, as the Valhalla motif is, tends to
draw the attention away from the melodic verse and toward the
orchestra.

Furthermore, its meaning is often not exact. Because it is not
positively identified by the words of the melodic verse, the identification tag by which it is known frequently varies. Those motifs
which originate in the orchestra often are given different names
by different interpreters. The motif to which we have referred as
Alberich's hatred is a case in point. It has other names, Envy,
Nibelung's Work of Destruction, Annihilation of the Gods, and
others. The discrepancy becomes much greater with the motifs

of the later works, as we shall see. Wagner himself sometimes gives varying connotations to this kind of orchestral leitmotif by his subsequent use of it. The Valhalla motif is employed in *The Valkyrie* to refer, not to Valhalla, but to Wotan. The Compact motif is later used to refer to Wotan's spear (the symbol of his duty as the keeper of compacts) and, occasionally, even for Wotan himself. The motif associated with Freia, and particularly the second half of it, called by some a Flight motif, defies positive identification, because of the various uses to which Wagner later put it.

Frequently a motif is used only as a kind of musical identification for a person or object and is repeated whenever that person appears or the name of the object is mentioned in the dialogue, where no actual reminiscence is involved. The technique does establish a relationship between word and tone or between stage picture and tone, but it is a much weaker device and does not strengthen the synthesis in the manner that the other motifs do.

It is apparent from the above discussion that leitmotif plays a much more significant role in the Wagnerian drama from this point on than ever before. A comparison of figures will serve to emphasize the difference. *Lohengrin* contains six principal motifs, the Lohengrin motif appearing the largest number of times, sixteen. The *Rhinegold* contains approximately twenty-six motifs of primary importance, and at least as many secondary ones. The Ring motif appears in *Rhinegold* alone fifty-one times. The Loge motif occurs thirty-five times.

Wagner required in *Opera and Drama* that motifs of reminiscence be used only at moments when the emotional level of the melodic verse falls to a point where its relationship with ordinary speech is most evident; that is to say, when it makes its appeal primarily to the intellect. At these moments, the motifs in the orchestra were to keep the emotional level high. His exact words are, "The orchestra is the medium for maintaining the unity of expression at all times. Wherever, for the purpose of defining the dramatic situation more clearly, the word-tone language of the actors must . . . descend to the point where it reveals its kinship with the language of daily life as a medium of intellect, the orchestra compensates for this by its ability to convey the reminiscences and forebodings musically, so that the awakened feeling remains in its uplifted mood." (W.S., IV, 199) When the melodic verse again attains its customary emotional intensity, the motifs are to be replaced by the orchestra's other function, harmonic elucidation. "These moments . . . withdraw into the background as soon as the individual again advances to the full expression of the melodic verse." (W.S., IV, 200)

This principle is completely ignored by Wagner in practice. There is not the slightest attempt to adhere to it. The motifs are used profusely in conjunction with the most highly emotional utterances of the characters, whereas the less impassioned moments, especially the narrative speeches, are generally accompanied by fewer, rather than more, leitmotifs. In *The Rhinegold* this is particularly true of Fricka's words in Scene 2.

We see then that Wagner's leitmotif in practice resembles his theoretical motifs to only a limited extent. Even in *The Rhinegold* it is a less precise entity than it was theoretically intended to be. In the dramas to follow, the connection between melodic verse and leitmotif becomes more and more remote. More and more the motifs tend to originate in the orchestra. In *Parsifal*, all but one do so. We shall see that this development is paralleled by others which tend in the direction of a dissolution of the firm practical bonds uniting poetry and music and stage action.

Wagner never attained consistency in his musical underlining of gesture. He seems to have left it to his own artistic sense when to use it and when to refrain. For the most part, of course, the more striking movements and gestures are musically pictorialized, as for instance the swimming of the Rhine maidens, Alberich's clumsy attempts to reach them, the giants' powerful strides, Loge's sinuous movements. Sometimes quite specific gestures are pictorialized, as when Loge loosens Alberich's bonds in Scene 4. On the other hand, decisive movements such as Wotan's stepping on the frog into which Alberich has transformed himself are not musically portrayed.

In *The Rhinegold,* as later in *The Valkyrie,* Wagner is faithful to the letter of his theory in banning concerted singing. There is no simultaneous singing at all except in the case of the three Rhine maidens, who are never individualized, and who speak more or less as one person. It is of greatest interest to see how Wagner gradually relaxes more and more in the application of this principle in each succeeding work after *The Valkyrie.*

Of presentiments not much is to be said in the course of our discussion of Wagner's works. The theory attributed to them a more precise function than they ever assume in any of the works. It is, of course, Wagner's consistent practice to prepare each scene by music in the appropriate mood, and we come to expect this from him in the very nature of things. Analyses cannot show anything as definite, however, as with leitmotifs. The prelude to *The Rhinegold,* where the mighty Rhine is gradually evoked musically in a way which makes the actual scene really the fulfillment of an awakened expectation, is perhaps the most striking example in all of Wagner, perhaps in all music. The Valhalla theme and the theme of the Nibelungs might possibly be classed as motifs of presentiment, since they appear before their counterpart on the stage. However, in their subsequent appearances, they function exactly as do all the other motifs, and no significance attaches to their having occurred shortly before Valhalla and the Nibelungs actually appear. In general, the transformation music between the scenes of *The Rhinegold* is less of an emotional preparation of what is to follow than a transition from one scene to the other, parallel to the visual transformations called for in the score, but only feebly executed in most performances, including those at Bayreuth.

chapter ten

The Valkyrie

IN THE VALKYRIE Wagner's new *Gesamtkunstwerk* approaches perfection. It is in all ways a richer, more beautiful, more satisfying work of art than *The Rhinegold*. Surely the subject matter had a great deal to do with this difference. It is easier to wax eloquent over the love of Siegmund and Sieglinde than it is over Loge's schemes for outwitting Alberich in order to rescue Wotan from his unwelcome bargain with the giants. Nor is there any doubt that Mathilde Wesendonck had something to do with it. The manuscript of the first act is decorated with code messages like "I.l.d.gr!!" ("Ich liebe dich grenzenlos"—"I love you boundlessly"), which indicate that Wagner was in the ideal mood for composing the love scenes between Sieglinde and Siegmund.

I am arguing in this book that there is a reciprocal influence between theory and practice. It is Paul Bekker's bold thesis in *Richard Wagner, His Life in his Work* that Wagner's life and work stand in a similar reciprocal relationship, that Wagner frequently reached a point where further creative work was dependent on further experiences and that Wagner actually went out looking for the experience which was necessary for the next stage of his creative activity. The thesis is expertly argued for Wagner's entire career, and there is no better example of this than the juxtaposition of his love for Mathilde Wesendonck and the love music in *The Valkyrie*. This would seem to make Wagner a *Gesamtkünstler* par excellence!

Whatever the influences, the music is decidedly more prominent in *The Valkyrie*. This increase in the importance of music brings the poetic-musical synthesis to its most perfect balance. There are no more instances of the kind in *The Rhinegold*, where

the musical line contributed very little to the total effect of the
word-tone phrase (see p. 83). Yet the music is still under strict
control from the *Opera and Drama* point of view, particularly in
Act I, where the melodic verse approaches perfection. In fact,
everything is in adjustment. Nowhere in all of Wagner's dramas is
there a more consummate balance of parts. Act I of *The Valkyrie*
is the finest creative parallel to the theory of *Opera and Drama*.
In this act, each gradation of word-tone balance and synchronization of music and action which is needed evokes from Wagner
the perfect synthesis, with the result that there is not a moment
when the blending seems less than ideal.

The point at which the melodic line is most subordinate to the
poetic verse is in Sieglinde's narrative of the sword. At times during this narrative, the accompaniment fades away to almost nothing and the vocal melody is relatively inconspicuous:

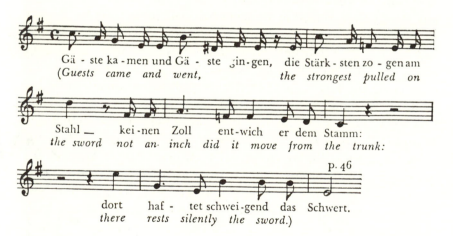

Nevertheless, even such a simple melodic phrase as "Gäste kamen,
und Gäste gingen" has an undeniable beauty of its own which
makes the force of the melodic element felt as an emotional expansion of the mood underlying the verse, with the result that the
two elements, word and tone, seem as one, a genuine synthesis.

Lyric passages, where the music justifiably takes a more conspicuous part in the word-tone balance, contain also the consummate blend of tone and word which gives a feeling of true musical-
poetic synthesis:

Win - ter-stür - me wi-chen dem Won - ne-mond,___ in
(*Winter's storms yield to the moon of May,* *in*

mil - dem Lich - te leuch-tet der Lenz;___ auf
soft light gleams the spring; *in*

lin - den Lüf - - - ten, leicht und lieb - - - lich,
balmy breezes, *light and lovely,*

P. 53

Wun - der we - bend er sich wiegt;
weaving miracles it sways;)

The music here is the ideal tonal expression of the lyric mood of the poetry. There is complete coordination between the two; the gently swaying rhythm of the melody and the verse is an esthetic evocation of the atmosphere of the spring night; at the same time, both verse and melody express the quiet lyricism of Siegmund's love for Sieglinde. The balance is delicately maintained. The slight touch of added exuberance expressed in the verse by "Wunder webend" is rendered melodically by the corresponding slight climactic effect of the high F.

Even at more discordant moments, particularly when the rugged Hunding speaks, esthetic beauty underlies the melodic and poetic irregularity of the menacing phrases. When Hunding notices the likeness between Siegmund and Sieglinde, for example, he sings in an aside:

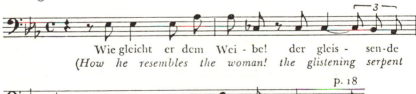

Wie gleicht er dem Wei - be! der gleis - sen-de
(*How he resembles the woman! the glistening serpent*

p. 18

Wurm glänzt auch ihm aus dem Au - ge.
gleams also from his eye.)

The dark quality of the melodic line brings out the ominous implication behind the verse. The effectiveness of these lines rests to a considerable extent in the way the intonation closely parallels the sense of the words. His surprise at how the two resemble each other is caught to perfection in the musical line. The treatment of "der gleissende Wurm" has also just the right quality of suspicion, distrust, and puzzlement.

At least one longer passage is necessary in order to show the amazing flexibility of the melodic line in accommodating itself to the varying moods expressed by the poetic verse. Siegmund sings the following, when he is left alone, weaponless, before the fire, after having been recognized as an enemy by Hunding and challenged to combat on the following morning:

der mich nun Sehn-sucht   zieht,   die mit   süs - sem Zau-ber mich
to whom now longing draws me, who with sweet magic over-

sehrt,   im   Zwan -   ge hält   sie der Mann,   der
comes me, in bondage she is held by the man, who

mich   wehr - lo - sen   höhnt,   Wäl - se!   Wäl - se!
now taunts me, defenseless as I am Waelse! Waelse!

Wo   ist mein Schwert? Das star - ke Schwert, das im Sturm ich
Where   is my sword? The strong sword, that I am to

schwän -   ge,   bricht   mir   her - vor   aus der
wield in storm,   when there breaks forth   from my

p. 37

Brust,   was   wü - tend   das Herz   noch hegt?
breast what my raging heart still harbors?)

Prepared by an ever increasing urgency in the twenty-eight bars
of orchestra music which precede this excerpt, Siegmund's pent-up
emotions burst forth at (*1*), in his despair of ever finding the sword
promised him by Wälse. At (*2*), his mood changes to one of help-
lessness and dejection. The melody expresses this by a certain dull,
colorless, immobile quality, in contrast to the agitation of the
previous phrase. At (*3*), a gentleness and charm appear in the
melody (the modulation to B♭ major contributes to this effect)
as Siegmund's thoughts turn to Sieglinde. At (*4*), the sweetness of
the reminiscence is clouded by the awareness of all that stands in
the way of his awakening love. The melodic line is more urgent,

it pulsates with greater excitement, and thus forms a transition to section (5), where Siegmund openly expresses his longing for her. This phrase is quicker, more agitated, than the preceding one. The exaggerated skip on "Sehnsucht" produces a strained "long-ing" effect. At (6), there is a return to more block-like intervals, a certain strait-laced quality in the melodic line denoting her "bond-age." All this has been a gradual preparation for the despairing outburst at (7), where Siegmund, in his great need, cries to Wälse to send him the promised sword. The suppressed fury of the final section (8) is realized by the irresistible drive of the melodic line, chopped into forceful rhythmic fragments and swiftly progressing upward in pitch to the climax on the top G.

In spite of the variation of mood in the eight sections, there is a feeling of unity. The declamation is perfect, melodic and poetic rhythm are identical. Verse accents are without exception empha-sized by pitch stress, rhythmic accentuation and the various other melodic means Wagner outlined in *Opera and Drama*. Alliteration in the verses adds to the total effect ("Weib—wonnig"; "entzückend —zehrt"; "Sehnsucht zieht—süssem Zauber"; "hält—höhnt"; "Schwert—Sturm—schwänge"), and the continuity of the entire section joins these separate divisions to one another, forming a single, all-inclusive poetic-melodic alliterative unit. The orchestra provides a rich harmonic and coloristic background, without ever drawing attention away from the melodic verse, which retains un-challenged the center of attention. Constructed on numerous pat-terns such as these, without any lapses into a less homogeneous word-tone synthesis, Act I of *The Valkyrie* represents the ultimate in sustained word-tone balance within the melodic verse.

The verse form of *The Valkyrie* as a whole is based on the same principles as that of *The Rhinegold*. But the poem benefits from the more poignant action and the more passionate outpour-ing of emotion. In fact, it is from this work that one can best illus-trate the values of Wagner's new verse form, regarded, as it always should be, as part of the larger synthesis of the *Gesamtkunstwerk*. The extreme concentration of color words which themselves have a strong emotional impact, and the relative absence of neutral words which the music could do nothing with, in phrases like the following, give the music an extraordinary potential which Wag-

ner was quick to exploit. It is a question whether any other verse
form would be as fully satisfying for Wagner's purpose.

> Littest du Schmach und schmerzte mich Leid,
> war ich geächtet und warst du entehrt,
> freudige Rache lacht nun den Frohen!
> Auf lach ich in heiliger Lust,
> halt' ich dich Hehre umfangen,
> fühl' ich dein schlagendes Herz!   (*Walküre*, 50–52)

> (If you suffered outrage and sorrows tortured me,
> if I was outlawed and you were dishonored,
> joyful revenge laughs now for the happy ones!
> I laugh out in sacred joy,
> when I hold you, sublime one, in my embrace,
> when I feel your beating heart!)

Alliterative contrasts, ideal for musical interpretation, are in-
numerable:

"gehrt' ich nach Wonne, weckt' ich nur Weh!"   (*Walküre*, 27)
("If I longed for delights, I awakened only woe")

"was ich liebe, muss ich verlassen, morden, wen je ich minne"
                                                        (*Walküre*, 125)
("What I love I must forsake, murder whom I have ever loved")

"so jung und schön erschimmerst du mir: doch wie kalt und hart
     erkennt dich mein Herz"   (*Walküre*, 164)
("So young and radiantly beautiful you appear to me, but how cold
     and hard my heart knows you to be")

"der Traurigen kos't ein lächelnder Traum"   (*Walküre*, 173)
("the sad one is caressed by a smiling dream")

"freiester Liebe furchtbares Leid, traurigsten Mutes mächtigster
     Trotz"   (*Walküre*, 271)
("freest love's fearful suffering, saddest courage's most mighty defi-
     ance")

Alliterative parallels are as numerous:

"Brünstig geliebter, leuchtender Bruder"   (*Walküre*, 149)
("passionately loved, resplendent brother")

"Nicht sehre dich Sorge um mich: einzig taugt mir der Tod"
                                                        (*Walküre*, 218)
("Let not worry for me consume you: death alone is suitable for me")

"Die alles weiss, was einstens war, Erda, die weihlich weiseste Wala"
(*Walküre,* 114)
("She who knows all that ever has been, Erda, the wisest Wala")

Acts II and III are not without occasional lapses, where the
verse dominates the music as we saw it do in *The Rhinegold,* or
where the music runs roughshod over the other aspects of the synthesis. In the following from the scene between Wotan and Fricka
in Act II, the musical line of the first seven measures is too disjointed and unsymmetrical to create the feeling that it is the musical counterpart of the verses. The last four measures show the
contrast, for in these the melodic line assumes more symmetry and
a greater degree of importance and the feeling of smooth word-tone
synthesis returns:

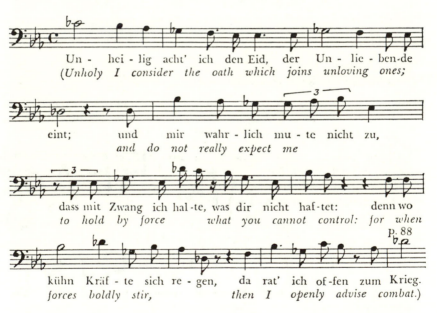

Looking toward Wagner's future development, it is noteworthy
that there is in *The Valkyrie* at least one scene and probably two
where the progress of the drama is held up for the purpose of
musical portrayal. The famous "Ride of the Valkyries," opening
the third act, is a scene of over two hundred measures, much of it
concerted singing by the eight Valkyries, in which the music is
clearly the overwhelmingly dominant element and the other as-

pects of the drama are temporarily subordinated to it. More frankly musical scenes occur in the later works, but this scene gives us the first unmistakable sign of the tendency which is eventually to cause Wagner to disregard more and more the principles of word-tone balance he set forth in *Opera and Drama*. Brünnhilde's first entrance, at the beginning of Act II ("Hojo-to-ho!"), is another, less extensive scene where the music is given a prominence which Wagner did not countenance in his theory.

Musical pictorializations of individual words, already noted in *The Rhinegold*, are abundant in *The Valkyrie*. With the general increase in the importance of music in the word-tone synthesis, it is natural that the pictorializations become more elaborate and more numerous. Many of them are so integrated into the action that they cannot be illustrated out of context. The music which accompanies Sieglinde's words in Act I, "O still! lass mich der Stimme lauschen: mich dünkt ihren Klang hört' ich als Kind" ("Quiet! let me listen to the voice: I think I have heard its sound as a child") (*Walküre*, 66), is one example. By the combination of the vocal line and the orchestra accompaniment, a very pronounced musical pictorialization of Sieglinde's searching in her mind for some memory of her childhood is produced. Of the many briefer pictorializations, the following are typical:

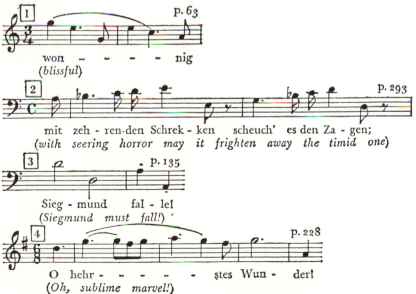

Wagner makes frequent use in *The Valkyrie* of wide skips (such as the minor ninths in the fifth example) to express agitation. A similar principle is involved in the last example. The awkward skips, which break into an otherwise chromatic ascent, depict the derision with which Siegmund addresses these scornful words to Brünnhilde. In the sixth example, it is the exaggerated emphasis on the rhythm, aided by the orchestral accompaniment, which portrays the biting sarcasm with which Wotan describes Brünnhilde's ignominious fate. Comparison of these examples with the ones taken from *The Rhinegold* (see pp. 87–88) will make clear how much more enterprising Wagner has become in his melodic pictorializations of individual words.

In *The Valkyrie* Wagner is more consistent in his musical treatment of alliterative verses. There are seventeen clear cases in *The Rhinegold* where musical alliteration extends the force of the alliterative verses. There are many more in this work. Whether small units or large, parallel or contrasting, the melody seldom misses an opportunity offered by the verse:

The alliterative contrast, of course, is between "mutig" and "müd'," although the sense of the entire first verse contrasts with the second. The "courageous" character of the first is subtly suggested by the strong dominant on the accented down beat (over a tonic F major $\frac{6}{4}$ chord in the orchestra). The C♮ quarter note is a higher pitch, and a longer note than any in the preceding section of three measures, and the decisiveness of the tonic chord which underlies the whole measure is in contrast with the more sinuous quality of the dominant seventh upon which the vocal line of the preceding three measures is built. The weaker effect of the verse containing "müd'" is obtained by avoiding the accented down beat and by moving the accompanying harmony to a dominant seventh under the A♮ of the melody, which belongs to the previous chord.

Extension of alliterative relationship to include the "b," "l," "d," and "g" alliterations of the following verse into one larger unit is accomplished by the melodic line, which produces a cumulative "dark" effect throughout the entire twelve bars:

da bleicht die Blü - te, das Licht ver - lischt;
(now fades the blossom, the light grows dim;

näch- ti-ges'Dun-kel deckt mir das Au - ge: tief in des' Bu - sens
night's darkness covers my eyes: deep in my breast

Ber - ge glimmt nur noch licht - lo - se Glut.
glows but a lightless gleam.)

p. 42

A similar unit is illustrated in the example on page 101.

The orchestra is more prominent in *The Valkyrie* than it was in *The Rhinegold.* In fact, it advances in importance perceptibly with each succeeding drama, in strictly chronological order, from *The Rhinegold,* through *The Valkyrie, Siegfried, Tristan and Isolde, The Mastersingers,* and *Twilight of the Gods,* to *Parsifal.* In *The Valkyrie* richness of orchestral texture and harmonic complexity are noticeably greater, and the subordination of orchestra to voice is somewhat less secure, although there is still no doubt about the fundamental dominance of the melodic verse. The harmonic support by the orchestra is more brilliant, but it is not so much so that it ceases to be support and becomes a competitor.

The tendency of the leitmotifs to disengage themselves from the melodic verse is more pronounced in *The Valkyrie,* but they are still used functionally. With the next work, *Siegfried,* the leitmotifs become so thoroughly orchestral, and are used so frequently, that it becomes impossible any longer to consider them functional reminiscences. Eighteen important new leitmotifs are added in *The Valkyrie,* and twenty-one of the twenty-six from *The Rhinegold* reappear. The Love motif occurs most often, fifty times, with the motif of Wotan's Anger second, occurring thirty-five times. The Sword motif, first heard in *The Rhinegold* (only twice there), occurs in *The Valkyrie* forty-one times. These figures do not include immediate identical repetitions. Thus, the Valkyrie motif is considered as appearing once in the opening scene of Act III, although it is heard there dozens of times.

An even smaller proportion of the new motifs is derived from the vocal line than was the case in *The Rhinegold.* Thirteen originate in the orchestra, and only five as part of the melodic verse. I have already discussed the fact that the motifs derived from the melodic verse, because of their inherent precision, contribute greatly to the unity and are a factor in maintaining the balance between the conceptual and the musical, and those not so derived swing the balance sharply in favor of the music, since they have no direct connection with the word (see pp. 93 ff.). The exact meaning of the five motifs derived from the melodic verse is quite apparent. As Brünnhilde sings in Act III, for instance, "Den hehrsten Helden der Welt hegst du, O Weib, im schirmenden Schoss" ("The noblest hero in the world you carry, oh woman, in your sheltering womb") (*Walküre,* 226), the melodic line automatically becomes the musical symbol for Siegfried. In the final scene, when Brünnhilde pleads with Wotan to surround her with frightening horrors, "dass nur ein furchtlos freiester Held hier auf dem Felsen einst mich fänd' " ("so that only a fearless free hero here on the rock should find me") (*Walküre,* 286), the identical melodic line is used. The emotional reminiscence, already present in the words, is immeasurably strengthened by the appearance of this motif in the melodic line. The listener's attention is directed back to the former scene between Brünnhilde and Sieglinde in a manner, and on an emotional plane, which would be otherwise impossible. The motif again appears as the melodic line to the final words of the drama, sung by Wotan, "Wer meines Speeres Spitze fürchtet, durchschreite das Feuer nie!" ("Who fears the point of my spear shall never penetrate the fire!") (*Walküre, 302*).

Commentators on Wagner seem never to judge the motifs at their true value. One frequently reads statements to the effect that the Siegfried motif occurring at this point reveals conclusively that it is to be Siegfried who will pierce the flames (in the next drama). Ernest Newman says, "Wagner, by making him sing the words to the Siegfried motive, once more plays the part of prophet to us." (S.G.O., I, 221) Ernest Hutcheson in *A Musical Guide to the Ring of the Nibelung* (p. 80) says, "For truly, it is Siegfried who is destined to defy the sacred spear, and brave the belt of flame." If the function of these motifs were solely to give away in advance what is to happen in the next drama, they would have far less justification for existence than they do possess. The presence of the motif here performs the ideal function of the motif of reminiscence. It reveals that Wotan is thinking of Siegfried and frames that revelation in terms of an emotional reminiscence, linking it with the original word-tone synthesis which contained the words, "den hehrsten Helden der Welt," etc. It thereby relates a key emotional point from the past to a similar moment in the present. In this case, it is not merely an intensification of a reminiscence already inherent in the poetic verse, for the words are not definite enough to reveal any reference to Siegfried. It is the leitmotif alone which provides the additional perspective.

On the other hand, at least four of the orchestral motifs are quite indefinite in meaning. One, which occurs frequently in the two dramas to follow, is identified by Edward Terry in *A Richard Wagner Dictionary* as "The Sorrow of the Volsungs"; by Newman (S.G.O., I, 190) as "Wälsung's Woe"; while Hutcheson calls it the motif of "Sieglinde." "Sieglinde" is the name usually given to an entirely different motif, as for example by F. P. Patterson in *The*

Leit-motives of Der Ring des Nibelungen, "Second Night, Die Walküre"; while both Terry and Richard Aldrich (*A Guide to the Ring of the Nibelung*) refer to this motif as "Sieglinde's Sympathy." Hutcheson calls it "Pity"; and Albert Lavignac (*Le Voyage Artistique à Bayreuth*), "Compassion." A third motif is referred to variously as "Anger" (J. Burghold, *Der Ring des Nibelungen von R. Wagner*); "Need of the Gods" (Patterson); "Wotan's Anger" (Lavignac); "Wotan's Grim Humor" (Aldrich); and "Wotan's Dejection" (Newman).

Wagner shares in the blame for these divergent interpretations. The absence of a firm conceptual association led him to greater freedom in their use. He is not always consistent in the subsequent repetitions of these motifs and various interpreters of leitmotif have given them one tag or the other, depending on which repetition they considered most important. This dilemma could not have arisen if the motifs had always been drawn from the melodic verse, for they would then have been immediately and infallibly identified.

In rare instances, Wagner is even guilty of inconsistent use of a leitmotif which is drawn from the dialog. There seems to be no explanation, for instance, for his use of the Renunciation theme (see p. 91, second example) at the end of Act I for the words of Siegmund, "Heiligster Minne höchste Not, sehnender Liebe sehnende Not" ("Sacred love's greatest need, languishing love's languishing need") (*Walküre,* 71). But this fact does not cause any uncertainty in the identification of the motif. That is so firmly fixed by the words with which it first appeared that no one would be tempted to give it a different name.

The absence of concerted singing in *The Valkyrie* should be mentioned, because this is the last work about which this can be said. Except for the ensemble of the Valkyries at the opening of Act III, no two voices ever sing at the same time, not even in the most impassioned parts of the love "duet" between Sieglinde and Siegmund in Act I. From *Siegfried* on, every drama contains a considerable amount of concerted singing.

chapter eleven

Schopenhauer

FROM THE FALL of 1854 for the rest of Wagner's life, Arthur Schopenhauer became one of the most pervasive influences over his thinking, writing, and composing. Introduced to the philosopher's work by his friend, the poet Herwegh, he read all of *The World as Will and Idea,* as well as the *Parerga and Paralipomena.* By this time, he was in exactly the frame of mind for Schopenhauer's classic doctrines of pessimism and renunciation. His sense of adventure at having broken with the past and embarked on a revolutionary new course had given way to disappointment and discouragement. His great work, the *Ring,* was obviously going to encounter almost insuperable difficulties, if indeed it ever was to be finished and produced. His main source of income (aside from begging and borrowing) was royalties, principally from *Tannhäuser* and *Lohengrin,* which he had long since left behind him, and performances of which, though frequent, he had ample reason to believe were mostly bad. There were other domestic difficulties, major and minor.

On February 5, 1855, Wagner wrote to August Röckel, "I confess that I had reached a point in my life where only Schopenhauer's philosophy could be completely adequate and decisive. By accepting without reservation his very, very serious truths I have satisfied my inner needs most fully, and although this has taken me in a direction which is widely divergent from my former course, it alone was consonant with my deeply suffering conception of the nature of the world." (W.A.R., 52)

Of more importance for us, and I believe intrinsically of far greater significance, is the influence on Wagner of Schopenhauer's esthetics, particularly his unique view of music, which Wagner found too fascinating to resist, even though it ran counter to the major premises of his own theory. In the first pages of Book III of *The World as Will and Idea,* Schopenhauer identifies the Kantian *Ding an sich,* which he accepts as the ultimate reality behind the world of phenomena, as the metaphysical will, and sets up the eternal Ideas or unchanging forms of Plato as direct objectifications of this will, a kind of generic mid-point, independent of the laws of time, space, and causality, between the will and the phenomenal world. All forms of art except music, argues Schopenhauer later in Book III, are revelations in terms of phenomena of these eternal Ideas. Music alone is independent of the world as representation, since it does not derive its material from phenomena, and is an objectification, not of the Ideas, but of the metaphysical will itself. "Music, having no connection with the Ideas, is independent also of the phenomenal world. . . . Music is by no means, like the other arts, an image of the Ideas: but an image of the will itself, whose objectification the Ideas are. It is for this reason that the effect of music is so much mightier and more penetrating than that of the other arts; for these speak only of the shadow, music however of the essence." (A.S., I, 340) Music is to Schopenhauer then a kind of eternal Idea itself; in fact, he asserts that music could exist even if the phenomenal world were nonexistent.

This glorification of music as a super-art Wagner found irresistibly fascinating. He not only accepted it fully, but it so affected his views on art and his creative faculties that one can say he was never again the same as an artist after having read it. I do not believe it is overstating the case to say that Wagner's creative work from this time on takes a new direction and that everything subsequently produced would have had a very different form if Schopenhauer's influence had been absent. The musician in him was suddenly given a new lease on life. From *The Flying Dutchman* on we have seen him more and more carefully and consciously subordinating music to the other phases of his art synthesis. We have seen further how this tendency reached its peak in *The Art-Work of the Future,* and how the adjustments made in *Opera and Drama* proved to be a kind of reversal of direction in favor of the music. Now a new powerful impetus to the release of music is added in the form of Schopenhauer's theory.

It is at once clear that the alignment of the arts on the principle of equality in a *Gesamtkunstwerk* "which is to include all
phases of art and in doing so to consume, to destroy each one, so
to speak, in favor of the total purpose of them all" (W.S., III, 60)
is incompatible with Schopenhauer's view of the exceptional position of music. Wagner must have been aware of this from the start,
because Schopenhauer spells out his rejection of a synthesis of the
arts in no uncertain terms. And indeed, he eventually tackled the
problem head on in *Beethoven,* where he formulated a new theory
of the *Gesamtkunstwerk* using Schopenhauer's view of music as its
starting point (see Chapter Fifteen). But in the meantime, the
philosopher's influence at first manifests itself in a less systematic,
if no less pervasive, way.

Whether Schopenhauer had any effect on *The Valkyrie* will always remain a moot point. The dates for the music are: Act I,
June 28 to September 1, 1854; Act II, September 4 to November
18, 1854; Act III, November 20 to December 27, 1854. The orchestration required an additional year and a half. Wagner first
read Schopenhauer in the autumn of 1854; he speaks briefly but
enthusiastically about him at the close of a long letter to Hans von
Bülow, dated October 26, 1854. (R.W.F., 164) A letter to Liszt in
December of that year contains the following: "Along with the—
slow—progress of my music I have been occupying myself exclusively with a man who is . . . like a gift from Heaven in my
loneliness. It is Arthur Schopenhauer, the greatest philosopher
since Kant." (W.L., II, 45) All of the references around this time
have to do with metaphysics and ethics, in particular Schopenhauer's doctrine of quietism, which attracted Wagner all the more
because he was beginning to be occupied with *Tristan.* It is not
until June 7, 1855 that we get the first clear evidence that Schopenhauer's metaphysics of music have brought a change in his attitude
toward the place of music in the drama. It occurs in a letter to
Liszt. "Music is actually the artistic proto-image of the world itself;
no error is possible here for the initiated." (W.L., II, 84)

In this same letter appears a striking revaluation of the final
movement of Beethoven's *Ninth Symphony,* which shows vividly
how powerful Schopenhauer's influence had already become. In
the *Opera and Drama* period Wagner had written that it was

Beethoven's intuitive act of musical-poetic synthesis in the final movement of the *Ninth* which paved the way for the ideal drama. In *The Art-Work of the Future* he had written, "Beethoven's last symphony is the redemption of music from its most individual element into universal art. It is the human gospel of the art of the future. Beyond it there can be no further progress, for only the perfected art-work of the future, universal drama, to which Beethoven has forged the artistic key, can be its successor." (W.S., III, 96) In *Opera and Drama* had appeared, "When he [in the final movement] with this simple, limited melody feels the poet's hand in his, he strides ahead, working in accordance with the spirit and form of the poem, to ever bolder and ever more varied tonal structure, to bring us at last miracles such as we never before conceived of, miracles like 'Seid umschlungen, Millionen' ['Be embraced, ye millions'], 'Ahnest du den Schöpfer, Welt?' ['Do you sense the creator, oh world?'], and finally, the clearly understandable combination of the 'seid umschlungen' with 'Freude, schöner Götterfunken' ['Joy, wonderful divine spark']—all of these arising out of the potentialities of poetizing tonal language." (W.S., IV, 150)

Now, after Schopenhauer, Wagner writes to Liszt in a very different vein: "The last movement of the *Ninth Symphony* with its choruses is decidedly the weakest part. It is important only historically, because it reveals to us in a very naive way the embarrassment of the real tone-poet who (after Hell and Purgatory) does not know how to portray Paradise." (W.L., II, 78–79) There can be no doubt that the new concept of music as a supreme art has brought about this change. Wagner never ceased thinking of Beethoven as his John the Baptist, as we shall have occasion to see in his late essay devoted to the great composer, but from this point on, his importance does not rest for Wagner, as it had done until now, in the word-tone synthesis in the final movement of the *Ninth*.

In an essay, "On Franz Liszt's Symphonic Poems," written in February 1857, during the composition of Act I of *Siegfried*, appears the first public statement implying Wagner's acceptance of Schopenhauer's metaphysics of music. "Hear my creed: music can never, regardless of what it is combined with, cease being the highest, the redeeming art. Its nature is such that what all the other arts only hint at becomes in it the most indubitable of certainties, the most direct and definite of truths." (W.S., V, 191) Wagner's first attempt to fit this new metaphysical role of music into the theory of art synthesis was not made until "Music of the Future" in 1861, two years after *Tristan and Isolde* was completed, and will therefore be discussed later, in Chapter Fourteen.

chapter twelve

Siegfried

WAGNER began the composition of *Siegfried* sometime between June and September 1856, therefore clearly after he had come under the influence of Schopenhauer. It is a fact that in this work the orchestra is considerably more prominent than in any previous work of Wagner's. It is richer in texture; the treatment of the leitmotif is more complex and more exclusively orchestral; and there is no longer the strict subordination of the orchestra to the vocal line which we have shown in *The Rhinegold* and *The Valkyrie*. It can scarcely be coincidental that this not insignificant alteration of the balance between the parts of the *Gesamtkunst-werk* occurs shortly after Wagner has given unmistakable evidence of interest in an esthetic which glorifies music as the greatest of the arts—as an art the effect of which is so powerful that it cannot be combined on a basis of equality with any other art. Attributing this change to the influence of Schopenhauer is the more plausible because we will be able to show that Wagner's alignment of the various elements of his synthesis, in both theory and practice, is more and more deliberately and fully assimilated to Schopen-hauer's views, until in *Beethoven* Wagner constructs a thoroughly Schopenhauerian theory of the synthesis of the arts, which serves well (as *Opera and Drama* decidedly does *not*) as a theoretical counterpart to the late works.

Though it is clear that Wagner was at heart more of a composer than he was a poet or dramatist, it is a fact that in *The Rhinegold* and *The Valkyrie* he had created two works in which the music, while unquestionably the dominant feature, is functionally sub-ordinate to the verse and action. The poetic-musical verse is the undisputed center of the dramatic structure, and the orchestra, although potentially the most powerful musical factor, is kept in check. Beginning with *Siegfried,* this relationship begins to break down, although the change in emphasis is at first not drastic, at least not in Acts I and II. (It will be remembered that there was an interval of twelve years between Acts II and III of *Siegfried,* so that the last act represents a later stage in Wagner's development.) They are still generally consistent with the *Opera and Drama* theory. Beside the fact that the new concept of the metaphysical role of music was a very recent acquisition, not yet assimilated in Wagner's mind to his theories of the ideal drama, there were also strong ties attaching *Siegfried* to the earlier theory. Its poem had been his first artistic creation after the long interval devoted to *The Art-Work of the Future* and *Opera and Drama,* and consequently the very first artistic exemplification of those theories. Its content was a continuation of the action of *The Rhinegold* and *The Valkyrie.* Only one character appears in it who has not already been seen in the two earlier works. Further, the thematic material to be drawn on in composing the music was rooted in the two preceding dramas. On the whole, therefore, it is still possible to consider *Opera and Drama* as the dominant theoretical influence on *Siegfried,* Acts I and II, while noting the deviations which herald a new esthetic position.

The poem, his first attempt at the new verse (see chronology on pp. 81–82), is not nearly as effective artistically as the poem of *The Valkyrie,* whether judged by Wagner's own or any other set of values. Its main components, as in all the *Ring* poems, are copious alliteration, irregular rhythm, and a high concentration of color words. Compact alliterative units on the pattern of the *Opera and Drama* theory, of which *The Valkyrie* contained many, occur considerably less often. For the most part, the alliteration is a more general poetic device which is not used to express parallels or contrasts:

> Da hast du die Stücken, schändlicher Stümper;
> hätt' ich am Schädel dir sie zerschlagen!
> Soll mich der Prahler länger noch prellen?
> Schwatzt mir von Riesen und rüstigen Kämpfen,
> von kühnen Taten und tüchtiger Wehr;
> will Waffen mir schmieden, Schwerte schaffen;

rühmt seine Kunst, als könnt' er 'was recht's:
nehm' ich zur Hand nun was er gehämmert,
mit einem Griff zergreif' ich den Quark!
Wär' mir nicht schier zu schäbig der Wicht,
ich zerschmiedet' ihn selbst mit seinem Geschmeid,
den alten, albernen Alp!   (*Siegfried*, 16ff.)

(There you have the pieces, disgraceful bungler;
if I had only shattered them on your skull!
Shall the boaster dupe me still longer?
He chatters to me of giants and vigorous battles,
of bold deeds and capable defence;
he wants to forge weapons, to make swords for me;
boasts of his skill, as if he could really do something:
when I take in my hand what he has hammered,
with one grip I shatter the piece of trash!
If the rascal were not so scurvy,
I would melt him down along with his trinkets,
the stupid old elf!)

Because the scene, action, dialog, and atmosphere of *Siegfried*, especially of Act I, are quite different from those of the two previous works, the poetic-musical verse is also much changed. The measured stateliness of the *Valkyrie* scenes gives way here to dialog and action which are crisp, rapid, scherzo-like. The melodic line reflects this mood by a corresponding liveliness and rapidity, expressing the impetuosity of young Siegfried, Mime's awkward attempts at cunning and craft, the furious bickering between Mime and Alberich. This contrasts markedly with the long flowing melodic lines which imbue *The Valkyrie* with a more lyric quality. It is essential to realize, however, in view of Wagner's later development, that this fact does not imply a relaxation of the word-tone principles of *Opera and Drama*. The kind of liveliness exhibited in parts of *Siegfried* is quite different from the technique later to be developed in *The Mastersingers*, where the dialog bears an entirely different relationship to the total work, as we shall subsequently see.

That the poetic-melodic verse in *Siegfried* is firmly rooted in the theory of *Opera and Drama* can be most clearly observed in illustrations from Siegfried's long scene in Act II, where he expresses his joy at being separated from Mime and speculates about his own father and mother. Here occur some of the most magnificent examples of lyric word-tone synthesis ever written by Wagner:

A-ber   wie sah mei-ne Mut - - ter wohl
(*But   how did my mother look?*

aus?   Das   kann ich nun gar nicht mir
              That I can scarcely imagine!

den-ken!   Der Reh-hin-din gleich   glänz - ten ge -
              Like the doe   gleamed surely

wiss   ihr'_ hell schim-mern-de Au - gen?   Nur noch viel
          her brightly shimmering eyes?   Only much more

p. 174

schö - ner!
beautifully!)

The orchestra accompaniment, pianissimo throughout, plays a variation of the Sieglinde motif from *The Valkyrie*, which also appears in the melodic line to the words, "Wie sah meine Mutter wohl aus?" The lines, "Das kann ich nun gar nicht mir denken," and the exquisitely delicate final verse, "nur noch viel schöner," are without accompaniment. The balance between word and tone is on a level with the best in *The Valkyrie*. There is no question but that the verse is the starting point for the entire word-tone combination. The music has been shaped to the poetic verse and interprets it, intensifying its inherent emotional potentialities. Melodic and poetic accents are matched throughout, and the two rhythms coincide exactly. The orchestra is subordinate.

More like the later melodic style of *Tristan and Isolde* is the following, wherein Siegfried's longing to see his mother is gorgeously summed up:

Ach, möcht' ich,   Sohn, mei ne Mut - - - ter ˙se - hen!
(*Oh, how I, her son, would like to see my mother!*)

Here Wagner magnificently expresses Siegfried's yearning by the broad extension and the crescendo on the vowel of "Mutter." We shall see that in *Tristan* this device is used to such a degree that the relationship with the verse is weakened, and it becomes a purely musical effect.

As in the Hunding scenes from *The Valkyrie,* where the ugly and sinister were magnificently treated, so also in *Siegfried* the menacing words of Alberich (Act II, Scene 1) are couched in terms that communicate the sense of evil, and of impending disaster, with great artistic intensity:

Denn fass'___ ich ihn wie - der einst in der Faust,   an -
(*For when I hold it again in my grasp,*   *not*

- ders als dum - me Rie - - sen üb' _____ ich ___ des
like the stupid giants will I use the power of the ring:

Rin - ges Kraft: dann zit - t're der Hel - - den e - wi - ger
               then tremble the eternal protector of

Hü - ter!   Wal - halls Hö - hen   stürm' ich mit Hel - las
heroes!   Walhalla's heights   I will storm with Hella's

p. 148

Heer: der   Welt___   wal - te dann ich!
hordes: the world I will rule then!)

Vowel extension is prominently used to sustain and to prolong the ominous atmosphere of Alberich's threats. The syncopation in the fourth, fifth, and sixth measures expresses his diabolical cunning. The Ring motif is woven into the vocal line from the fourth to the seventh measure, carrying with it a strong reminiscence of the original words, "Der Welt Erbe gewänne zu eigen wer aus dem Gold schüfe den Ring" ("The heritage of the world he would win who from the gold could fashion the ring"). The steady chromatic ascent creates a gradual intensification which is already inherent in the words. Word and tone reach the climax simultaneously on the high F♯ of "Welt." There is an unusually rich motival accompaniment. For four measures preceding this excerpt, and continuing through the first two measures of the example, is heard the strongly syncopated motif of Alberich's hatred from *The Rhinegold*. From the third to the seventh measure, the Ring motif is heard in the orchestra as well as in the vocal line. Below the words, "Der Helden ewiger Hüter," appears a suggestion of the Curse motif. What follows is accompanied by the Bondage motif. The measures immediately following this excerpt contain the grandiose theme of Alberich's dream of triumph.

In Act I, Siegfried's youthful impatience is contrasted vividly with Mime's sly attempts to pacify the boy by playing upon his sympathies. Both are combined in the following, sung by Siegfried:

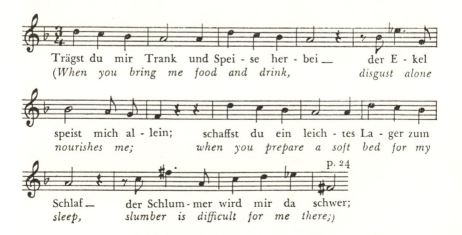

Trägst du mir Trank und Spei - se her - bei __   der E - kel
(*When you bring me food and drink,*   *disgust alone*

speist mich al - lein;   schaffst du ein leich - tes La - ger zum
nourishes me;   *when you prepare a soft bed for my*

Schlaf __   der Schlum - mer wird mir da   schwer;
sleep,   *slumber is difficult for me there;)*

p. 24

In the first half of each line, Siegfried is mockingly imitating the cajoling tones of Mime. Note the strong, regular, sentimental rhythm in both words and music. (When sung by Mime it usually contains grace notes as well.) The second half, in contrast, again in words as well as in music, is irregular in accent and rhythm, and expresses Siegfried's impatience at Mime's persistent attempts to sentimentalize his parental care.

There are some marvels of musical-poetic dramatic characterization in this work. In Act II, after Siegfried has slain Fafner, the scheming dwarf, Mime, approaches him with a draught that will render Siegfried unconscious and permit Mime to slay him with his own sword. Mime offers him the potion as a cooling drink to refresh him after his struggle with the dragon. But, having touched the dragon's blood to his lips, Siegfried has the power to see beneath Mime's dissembling. Try as he might to conceal his evil intentions by a tender solicitude, the truth will out, and Mime finds himself betraying his motives unwittingly. The word-tone synthesis conveys the tragi-comic effect of this scene brilliantly. Mime's most dire threats are set to the most cajoling sort of pseudo-friendly melodic line:

There is one passage in the first act where the music decidedly overbalances the poetry in the dialog: the famous "Song of the Forge," comprising the greater part of the concluding scene. This

very nearly approaches being an outright "aria" in a way we have
not seen in the early *Ring* dramas:

Des Bau -   mes Koh - le,   wie brennt _ sie kühn; wie
(*The   tree's   embers,*   *how   burn   they   boldly;   how*

p. 110

glüht _ sie hell _   und _   hehr! ___
glow   they   brightly   and   grandly!)

As in a traditional aria, the poetic line is not integrated beyond the
most general agreement in mood. The melody is constructed in
strict period form with a symmetry of its own that does not extend
to the verse. The latter is of little consequence in the total effect.
The sheer brilliance of the music is the conditioning factor for the
whole excerpt. This dominance of music in the melodic verse is,
of course, another transitional aspect pointing the way to *Tristan*.

To sum up, the melodic verse of *Siegfried* continues essentially
the same kind of word-tone balance that exists in *The Valkyrie*.
Just as in that work, it is the focal point of the drama. It is not
subordinate to the orchestra, as it becomes in *The Mastersingers*,
although, as will be shown below, the orchestra is no longer always
subordinate to it, as it was in *The Valkyrie*. Except in the instance
noted above, the melodic verse does not significantly indicate any
alteration in the balance of the components. *Siegfried* is the last
work about which this can be said. With *Tristan and Isolde* a new
relationship prevails.

It is in the orchestra that the transformation has taken place.
Beginning with *Siegfried,* the role of the orchestra in the works
of Wagner is permanently altered. The total mass of orchestral
effect is so great and so complex that it is no longer felt as a
harmonic support only but frequently assumes a position of equal
importance with the vocal melody. This growth in harmonic complexity cannot be attributed to the character of the drama. All
other conditions being equal, the picture of the youthful Siegfried,
especially in Act I, would demand a less intricate tonal pattern

than the grandiose scenes of *The Valkyrie*. The orchestral brilliance must therefore be attributed to an impulse, whether intuitive or conscious, to augment the proportionate role of the music in the drama. And in this Schopenhauer's influence can be seen.

The change in relationship can be illustrated in a very simple but striking way: the audience attending consecutive performances of the four *Ring* dramas finds that suddenly in *Siegfried* it becomes considerably more difficult to *hear* the singers, because of the tonal weight of the orchestra. Several aspects bearing on the relationship between the dialog, action and music will illustrate this change. *Siegfried* contains some magnificent examples of orchestral pictorialization. Such effects as the murmuring of the forest leaves, the grandiose musical evocation of fear, the bird calls, the forge music are striking instances of this. They alone, however, are no indication of a change in the function of the orchestra, for they find their parallel in similar portrayals in *The Rhinegold* and *The Valkyrie;* the rainbow, for example, or the storm, the Valkyries riding through the air, the magic fire. There occurs in *Siegfried,* however, an additional kind of orchestral pictorialization which has not been encountered before. Wagner rarely misses an opportunity for brief orchestral pictorializations of incidental effects, when the dialog or the action presents them. Such effects as the orchestra's description of the swinging of Fafner's tail (*Siegfried,* 164), of the hissing steam when Siegfried tosses the red-hot sword into the water (*Siegfried,* 114), of the placid, mirrorlike brook in which Siegfried has seen his image (*Siegfried,* 33), of fluttering wings of young birds (*Siegfried,* 30), of fish swimming (*Siegfried,* 33) are all incidental descriptions which grow out of the words of the dialog or out of the action but are not key dramatic elements. The occasion for their appearance is a more or less incidental mention of bird, fish, brook, or dragon in the dialog, and the pictorialization lasts for only a few measures. This technique gives added prominence to the orchestra.

In *Siegfried,* Wagner's use of the leitmotif too has shifted significantly. In *The Rhinegold* and *The Valkyrie,* the motifs were for the most part used only functionally to supplement and clarify the background of the dialog. In *Siegfried* (and in all of the succeeding works), the integration of orchestral motif with dialog is much less careful. The motifs occur so frequently, often two, sometimes three being woven together in one measure, that reminiscences, the function for which the motif of reminiscence was originally intended, are no longer possible. The motival interplay tends to become a contrapuntal interweaving with a purely musical significance.

In the whole of *The Rhinegold* there are 279 different occurrences of motifs. In *The Valkyrie,* a much longer work, there are 405. But in the first two acts alone of *Siegfried,* there are 452 occurrences of leitmotif. We have mentioned before that these figures do not refer to every repetition, but only to each one under at least slightly different circumstances; thus, for instance, the Forge motif, repeated in the final scene of Act I dozens of times, is counted as one statement of the motif. If every single repetition of motifs were counted, the figures for *Siegfried* would be in the thousands. *Siegfried* is thus clearly transitional from the functional leitmotif technique of *The Valkyrie* to the contrapuntal technique of *The Mastersingers,* where, as we shall see, contrapuntal interweaving of motifs is the rule.

There are numerous examples involving genuine reminiscence in *Siegfried* (see the references to the Ring and Curse motifs in the example on p. 123), but instances where the musical interplay of motifs in the orchestra becomes its own justification can also be found. Thus, for example, when the dying Fafner says to Siegfried, "Dein Hirn brütete nicht, was du vollbracht" ("Your brain did not conceive what you have accomplished") (*Siegfried,* 191), we hear simultaneously the Curse motif from *The Rhinegold,* the Love motif from Act I of *The Valkyrie,* and the Siegfried motif from Act III of *The Valkyrie.* There is a certain justification for each of these according to the principles of *Opera and Drama,* but simultaneous emotional reminiscence of three widely separated past moments is so cumbersome that it breaks down and gives way to recognition of the contrapuntal treatment of the three motifs as a musical device. Examples of this kind are not numerous in the first two acts of *Siegfried.* With Act III, to be discussed in a later chapter, and with *Twilight of the Gods,* the motival interplay is so complex that it would be hopeless to attempt to disentangle the motifs and search for functional reminiscence.

There are two other phases of leitmotif which indicate a deviation from the original *Gesamtkunstwerk* in the direction of greater independence for the music. Wagner begins in *Siegfried* to use the motifs without reference to their original word-tone connotation. There are at least twenty-one cases where a leitmotif is employed either inconsistently with the principles of *Opera and Drama* or with a very meagre word-tone justification. Such usage has a strong effect in breaking down the word-tone force and centering the attention on the music. It is also a fruitful source of confusion for the interpreters who attempt to name the motifs. Assuming that Wagner's treatment of leitmotif is uniform throughout all the *Ring* dramas, they try to find definitions which will fit all later cases as well as the earlier ones, and there are consequently many discrepancies. The fallacy is in assuming that Wagner's technique is invariable.

An illustration of this is Wagner's use of the motif of Wotan's farewell to Brünnhilde from the closing scene of *The Valkyrie*, when he rides away after his encounter with Alberich in front of Fafner's den. There has not been the remotest suggestion of anything that could call forth the motif at this moment. Yet it was originally derived from a musical-poetic line and has therefore a firm connotation. A great deal of ingenuity is needed and employed by those who attempt to account for this. Ernest Hutcheson solves the present instance by stating that "thoughts of Brünnhilde haunt Wotan wherever he roams," which point, if true, is just as irrelevant as the motif itself. A most ingenious interpretation concerns Wagner's use of an exact inversion of Siegfried's Horn Call (with a descending fifth instead of the ascending fifth, etc.) as he releases the bear which he has brought to frighten Mime and lets it run back into the forest. Hutcheson's justification of this inversion is: " 'Twas for Siegfried's pleasure he came to the cave; he goes back for his own." The necessity for such forced reasoning makes it obvious that a change in technique has been effected. It is more logical and more accurate to recognize that at this point Wagner was paying less heed to his original plan for synthesis and giving the musical aspect of the *Gesamtkunstwerk* more freedom. The consequences of not recognizing and distinguishing this change of attitude on Wagner's part is clearly shown in Ernest Newman's discussion of leitmotif in *Wagner As Man and Artist.* "It has to be admitted," he writes, ". . . that Wagner's use of the leitmotive presents some singularities and is at times open to criticism." (W.M.A., 284) Making no differentiation in Wagner's technique from *Siegfried* on, Newman reproduces numerous examples in the succeeding six pages of his book to show inconsistencies. But every single example comes from either *Siegfried* or *Twilight of the Gods,* where the functional use is no longer decisive.

All of the ten major leitmotifs in Acts I and II of *Siegfried* are orchestral in origin, adding still further to the musical independence of the orchestra. As in the previous works, this gives rise to uncertainty in their connotation. In *Tristan and Isolde,* the leitmotif technique is so changed that any attempt to analyze leitmotifs as motifs of reminiscence is doomed to failure.

chapter thirteen
Tristan and Isolde

TRISTAN AND ISOLDE is in many ways the ultimate among Wagner's works. He is on record as believing that it fulfills his theoretical requirements for a *Gesamtkunstwerk* more fully than any other, although we shall see in the next chapter that this statement should be interpreted with greater caution than it has been in the past. Wagner also said, "This work is more thoroughly musical than anything I have done up to now," an opinion which we can accept more unreservedly. One thing is certain; after struggling with the cumbersome complexities of the *Ring* plot, he found in *Tristan and Isolde* a story far more responsive to his particular needs. When we consider his theories of synthesis as in essence a plan for attaining the maximum degree of dynamic expressivity from music, we can point to *Tristan* as the perfect medium for this. There is little external action. The plot is extremely simple. The center of gravity, so to speak, is shifted to the inner psychology and emotions of the characters and these are portrayed for all they are worth by the music. It is surely true that in no other drama are "the depths of inner spiritual processes," as Wagner put it, so richly and fully portrayed as in *Tristan and Isolde;* and the most potent means for this revelation of inner emotions is the music.

The undercurrent of Schopenhauer influence comes to the surface in *Tristan,* and this not only in the frequently discussed Schopenhauerian language of the second act but more significantly in the role of music. The second act is one long symphonic poem with vocal duet, in which there is almost no action, and the words are little more than sonant carriers for the musical tones, without conceptual significance. All else is drowned in the dazzling splendor of the music, music more daring harmonically and coloristically than had ever before been written.

The very conception of the work coincides with Wagner's sudden discovery of Schopenhauer, and his letters give us abundant evidence that his enthusiasm for that philosopher was a constant spur to the composition of poem and music. Although the principles of synthesis from *Opera and Drama* are the basis for the work, and certain portions of the drama (particularly Isolde's narrative, the drinking of the love potion, and the great speech of King Marke) are as magnificent examples of the *Opera and Drama* synthesis as are to be found anywhere, it can be shown that in most of the work (from the drinking of the potion to the end), the music is so overwhelmingly dominant that what seems to be a synthesis on the basis of a three-fold relationship of words, music, and action is closer to a glorification of music as a virtually independent super-art. In the essay, "Music of the Future," written a year later, something quite similar occurs. Although Wagner intended it to be a review of the principles embodied in *Opera and Drama,* it is actually a metaphysical argument glorifying the role of music as an independent art form. We will discuss this essay in the next chapter.

In every phase *Tristan* is a step beyond the *Ring.* The poem, though it shares many characteristics with the *Ring* poetry, is even more highly concentrated and contains rhyme and assonance, in addition to a great deal of alliteration. Wagner had been scornful about rhyme in *Opera and Drama,* and his use of it here is a definite break with his theoretical position, yet perhaps not so much so as it might at first seem. He had rejected rhyme because it lent undue emphasis to the last syllable of the line, which often was thereby given a prominence it did not warrant conceptually or emotionally. With very few exceptions in *Tristan* the rhyming word is a key word in the sentence, and the rhyme is felt to be commensurate with its importance in the verse. Strengthening further this use of rhyme, he frequently used it as he did alliteration in the previous poems: for purposes of establishing emotional contrasts:

"mir erkoren, mir verloren"   (*Tristan,* 15)
("chosen by me, lost to me")

"da die Männer sich all' ihm vertragen, wer muss nun Tristan
   schlagen?"   (*Tristan,* 76)
("since the men all make peace with him, who is to strike Tristan
   down?")

"Unabwendbar ew'ge Not für kurzen Tod!"   (*Tristan,* 94)
("Inevitable eternal distress for quick death")

"seiner Treue frei'ste Tat traf mein Herz mit feindlichstem Verrat!"
                                                      (*Tristan,* 199)
("his loyalty's freest deed struck my heart with hostile treachery!")

or parallels:

"Dem Wunder aller Reiche . . . dem Helden ohne Gleiche!"
                                                      (*Tristan,* 17)
("The wonder of all realms . . . the hero without compare!")

"und heim nach Hause kehre, mit dem Blick mich nicht mehr
   beschwere!"   (*Tristan,* 35)
("and return home, no longer with his glance to disturb me!")

"O Wonne voller Tücke! O truggeweihtes Glücke!"   (*Tristan,* 104)
("Oh ecstasy full of treachery! oh treacherous happiness!")

Where the music comes most fully to the fore, as in most of Acts
II and III, and the words are little more than convenient syllables
to which the music can be sung, rhyme, with its emphasis on vowel
sounds, is more adaptable than alliteration, and we indeed find
that in Act II, the really "symphonic" act, the proportion of rhyme
is more than double what it is in the first.

Alliteration is used as in the *Ring* dramas to express parallels
and contrasts:

"wütendem Wirbel"   (*Tristan,* 10)
("raging whirlpool")

"grollende Gier"   (*Tristan,* 10)
("grumbling greed")

"O blinde Augen, blöde Herzen"   (*Tristan,* 40)
("oh blind eyes, foolish hearts")

"der Trank ist's, der mir taugt!" "der Todestrank!"   (*Tristan,* 54)
("this is the potion which suits me!" "the death potion!")

"tör'ger Treue trugvolles Werk"   (*Tristan,* 94)
("foolish loyalty's deceptive work")

"des kühnsten Mutes Königin, des Welten-Werdens Walterin"
(Tristan, 122)

("the queen of greatest courage, the ruler of the world's destiny")

In Acts II and III, alliterated words are often only sonant carriers of a musical line which is virtually independent of the words (see illustration below, p. 141).

The same is true of Wagner's use of concentrated language, which appears in its most potent form in *Tristan*. There are some powerful examples, such as the famous

> Mir erkoren,—
> mir verloren,—
> hehr und heil;—
> kühn und feig!—
> Tod geweihtes Haupt!
> Tod geweihtes Herz!   (*Tristan*, 15)

> (by me chosen,—
> by me lost,—
> splendid and noble,—
> bold and cowardly!—
> death-devoted head!
> death-devoted heart!)

or Tristan's oath of reconciliation (see illustration below, p. 138). Occasionally the concentration gets out of hand and Wagner uses language which it takes some effort to unravel:

> Befehlen liess' dem Eigenholde
> Furcht der Herrin ich, Isolde.   (*Tristan*, 19)

> (Commanded have to the vassal
> fear of his lady I, Isolde.)
> [I, Isolde, have ordered the
> vassal to show respect for his lady.]

Frequently the high concentration of emotion words serves, as do the rhyming vowels and alliterating consonants, as only a syllabic framework for a dominating musical line, so that the potentialities of the words themselves are lost, as in the lines from Act II:

> All' Gedenken,
> All' Gemahnen,
> heil'ger Dämm'rung hehres Ahnen
> löscht des Wähnens Graus
> welterlösend aus.   (*Tristan*, 164)

(All remembrance,
all recollection,
sacred dusk's noble foreknowledge
extinguishes thinking's dread
redeeming the world.)

Most of this is shown with the vocal line in the illustration on pages 142–43. There are many similar examples from the second and third acts.

In the portions of *Tristan* where a synthesis of word, tone, and stage action in the *Opera and Drama* sense exists, this synthesis is more intense than any in the preceding works. The poem itself is more powerfully concentrated, more highly charged emotionally. The stage action is stripped to essentials, shifting the attention to the psychology and emotion of the characters. The manner of synthesizing the poetic dialog with vocal melody in the melodic verse is also more intense. The following, an impassioned poetic-melodic line, is sung by Isolde shortly after the curtain rises:

Zu to - ben-der Stür - me wü - ten-dem Wir-bel
(*To raging storms' wild whirlpool*

treibt aus dem Schlaf dies träu - men-de Meer:
drive from its sleep this dreaming sea,

weckt aus dem Grund sei - ne grol - len-de Gier!
wake from the depths its grumbling greed!

Zeigt ihm die Beu - te, die ich ihm bie - te!   Zer-schlag' —
Show it the booty I offer!   *If it will*

p. 10

— es dies trot - zi -ge Schiff, des zer -schell - ten Trüm-mer ver-schling's!
shatter this defiant ship, the ruin's wreckage it may consume!)

In spite of the frenzied pitch of Isolde's emotion, the balance between word and tone is maintained. (Quite the opposite is true in
all similar cases in Acts II and III.) The verse and the melody together build up a gradual climax, with the melodic line progressing relentlessly upward, till the peak in word and tone is reached
simultaneously on the word "zerschlag'." The climax is further
accentuated by the dramatic measure-long pause immediately preceding it, a pause which is inherent in the sense of the words and
by the extended vowel on "zer*schlag*'," which prolongs the climactic moment. There are fully twenty-one powerful accents in
the verse, all of which are increased in force by functional musical
synthesis. In accordance with the principles of *Opera and Drama,*
the accents are placed on relatively more emphatic steps of the
tonal scale, on relatively more forceful beats of the measure, or on
higher pitches. The six or seven subdivisions into which verse and
melody can be separated progress to minor climaxes of their own.
Perfect coordination exists between word and tone. The tendency
toward wide skips is to be noted. As Wagner attempts to increase
the dramatic power of the vocal line, he tends toward more and
more daring use of wide skips, a trend which reaches its peak in
Kundry's narrative in Act II of *Parsifal.*

On a less highly emotional level is the following example from
Isolde's narrative:

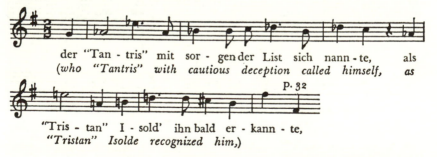

der "Tan - tris" mit sor - gen der List sich nann - te,   als
(who "Tantris" with cautious deception called himself,   as

P. 32

"Tris - tan" I - sold' ihn bald er - kann - te,
"Tristan" Isolde recognized him,)

There is a strong emotional contrast between the two lines of verse
because of the startling implications behind this revelation of her
discovery. The contrast is aided by the alliteration ("Tantris—
Tristan") and by the rhyme ("nannte—erkannte"). The melodic
line contributes to the contrast by a chromatic modulation from
lower, darker A♭ to brighter A♮, and by the melodic contour of

"Tantris" and "Tristan"; the ascending fifth of "Tantris" conveys a somewhat equivocal, uncertain feeling; the descending fifth of "Tristan" implies certainty, definiteness. The entire composition of the line is dictated by the meaning, and has significance only when related to that meaning. It could not stand as an independent musical phrase.

One of the most masterful word-tone syntheses of the entire drama occurs when Isolde reveals the power exercised over her by Tristan's gaze:

von sei -nem La - ger   blickt' er her,
(from his bed   he looked up,

nicht auf das ·Schwert,   nicht auf die Hand,
not at the sword,   not at my hand,

er sah — mir in die Au - gen.   Sei·nes E - - len - des
he looked into my eyes.   His misery

jam - mer-te mich;   das Schwert ich liess es fall - len!
grieved me;   the sword — I let it drop.)

P. 34

Here again, the blending of word and tone is functional. The melodic line is dependent upon the words to which it is united and serves the purpose of extending the emotional content of the words into the more expressive sphere of music. The disjointed character of the melodic line, for instance, is dictated by the sense of the words. (Such disjointedness is another device Wagner uses increasingly in his attempt to obtain the last ounce of expressivity from the vocal line. It too culminates in Kundry's narrative.) Even the beats of the measure on which each syllable is made to fall are minutely calculated to parallel the declamatory aspect of the verse. Especially effective is "das Schwert, ich liess es fallen." Vowel extension is used at the climax. The verb "jammerte" is brilliantly portrayed by the melodic contour.

It is invariably stated in guides to *Tristan* that the pointed appearance of the so-called "Love Glance" motif in the orchestra during the measure after the word "Augen" reveals the powerful effect on Isolde of Tristan's gaze. Actually, however, it is the melodic verse which most convincingly shows this. What the appearance of the motif in the orchestra might communicate has been far more impressively revealed by the preceding melodic line.

As a final example of parallelism between word and tone, here is Tristan's oath from Act I in full:

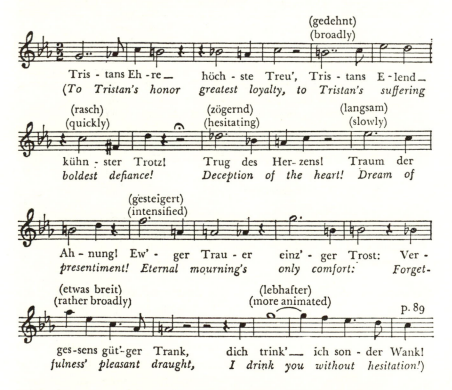

This is a most impressive illustration of what Wagner called musical alliteration. Beginning in the key of C minor on the first short phrase, the music goes through a cycle of modulatory harmonies which draw farther and farther away from the tonic C minor as the poetic expression expands. A return to C minor on the last phrase is magnificently effected by use of the Death motif, with its arresting A♭ to A♮ opening chords ("Vergessens güt'ger Trank"). The orchestra sounds the second half of the motif during the ensuing vocal pause—an F minor chord changing to a dominant seventh on G underneath the extended "trink'." The remainder of the vocal line completes the modulation through the dominant back into C minor. The use of the Death motif at this key point is of great emotional significance, establishing a vivid reminiscent link between this and the scene of the motif's first appearance. (See the quotation on p. 134 for words to the original Death motif.) This beginning and ending in C minor creates an enclosing musical bond which molds the entire oath into a single musical-poetic unit. Within it are smaller contrasting or parallel alliterative groupings. Of these concentrated poetic expressions, the first and third are bound together by alliteration ("Ehre—Elend"), as are also the second and fourth ("Treu'—Trotz"). The musical line also unites the first to the third and the second to the fourth by means of the melodic contour, thus strengthening the effect of the alliteration. At the same time, the ideas behind each meaningful expression are differentiated vividly by their musical treatment, the first contrasting with the second, and the third with the fourth. The phrases which follow build a gradual emotional crescendo to the climax on the last phrase.

Wagner's portrayal of the subtleties of anger, love, scorn, irony, sarcasm, excitement, etc. through the poetic-musical verse is nowhere else so consummate as in *Tristan*. The following is a magnificent example from Isolde's narrative:

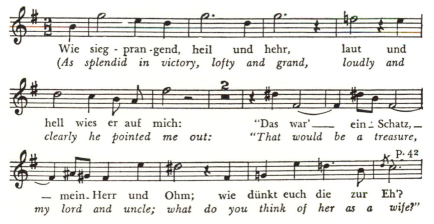

Wie sieg - pran -gend, heil   und hehr,   laut   und
(As splendid in victory, lofty and grand,   loudly and

hell wies er auf mich: "Das war'____ ein Schatz,__
clearly he pointed me out: "That would be a treasure,

— mein Herr und Ohm; wie dünkt euch die zur Eh'?
my lord and uncle; what do you think of her as a wife?"

p. 42

The first seven measures are sung in a mock heroic manner to a tune previously associated with praise of Tristan as a hero. The intense bitterness expressed by the ironic parody, "Das wär' ein Schatz" etc., is emphasized by the saccharine quality of the spuriously delicate melodic line, even to the grace note on "Eh'." Isolde's fury is aroused by these thoughts, and a few bars later on it reaches its climax on the harsh "mir *lacht*" of the following:

"ein Wink, ich flieg' nach I - ren - land.   I - sol - de, die ist
("a sign, and I'll rush to Ireland.   *Isolde will be*

p. 43

eu - er!   mir lacht das A - ben - teu - er!"
yours!   *I will enjoy the adventure!")*

In Act II, Marke shows how deeply wounded he has been by Tristan's infidelity in the words and music of a long speech which begins:

Mir   dies?   Dies Tris tan mir? ___   Wo - hin nun
(This to me?   This, Tristan, to me?   *Where   now*

Treu - e,   da Tris - - - tan   mich be - trog?   Wo - hin nun
is loyalty, since Tristan has betrayed me?   *Where   now*

Ehr' und ech - te Art, da al - ler Eh - ren Hort, ___ da Tris -
are honor and nobility, since the essence of honor, since

p. 200

- - tan   sie ver - lor?
Tristan has lost them?)

The irrational intervals of the first four bars are a revealing expression of Marke's incredulity at seeing Tristan as a traitor. The entire excerpt breathes the sorrow that overcomes Marke at the realization of Tristan's faithlessness. The melodic contour manages to convey all the pathos inherent in the verse.

All the preceding illustrations come from those portions of the work where a genuine synthesis in the *Opera and Drama* sense is present. When we turn to other parts (principally Acts II and III), we can illustrate a subtle alteration in the adaptation of those principles, which shifts the emphasis so strongly toward the music that both the poetry and the visual action fade into the background. This musical texture, unhampered, as it were, by any partnership, is broader and fuller in scope, richer and more magnificently opulent than any yet to come from Wagner's (or any one else's) pen. In fact, the love music from Act II, the famous "Liebesnacht," calls to mind Schopenhauer's view (see p. 150) that the text of an opera should always be in a subordinate position, so as to allow the music maximum freedom for its more profound revelations.

The principle of vowel extension has frequently been illustrated in earlier chapters. In Acts II and III of *Tristan* often the syllables thus extended are prolonged to such a degree that the conceptual meaning is submerged, and little remains but pure tone:

Ein - - sam wa - chend in __ der Nacht,—
(*Alone watching in the night,*

wem __ der Traum __ der Lie - - be lacht, __
on whom the dream of love smiles,)

p. 169

At a deliberate tempo, with an elaborate orchestral accompaniment, and sung from behind the scenes, the words have no effect. The passage is a magnificent lyric moment but one to which the word does not contribute.

A similar instance is the climax of the love duet:

These two examples, and many others which I could give, are not a reversion to the traditional disregard of the words which existed before Wagner. The vestiges of functional word-tone relationship are still there, the extension is made nominally to prolong the expression inherent in the words (this is evident especially in the last example, the melodic line ecstatically expressing "höchste Liebeslust"), but it is stretched beyond its farthest limit in the *Opera and Drama* sense.

Similarly, the principles of speech condensation, alliteration, and rhyme, all contained in the single example below, lose their significance because of the dominating position of music in the word-tone picture:

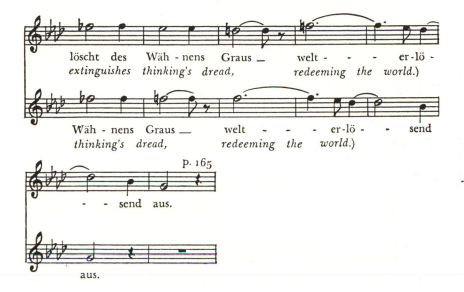

Not only are Tristan and Isolde singing simultaneously, but Isolde's words trail one full measure behind Tristan's. As a consequence, of course, the musical pattern dominates. The second act duet contains many such passages of free canonic imitation. We have seen that in *The Rhinegold, The Valkyrie* and Acts I and II of *Siegfried* actual duet singing does not occur at all. In those works, the spirit as well as the letter of *Opera and Drama* is fulfilled. Here, where music has slipped away from the confines of a three-fold synthesis, we find concerted singing also in evidence. A comparison of the love scene from Act I of *The Valkyrie* with that of *Tristan* illuminates vividly the alteration in technique. There is not a single bar of duet singing in the former. From *Tristan* on it appears in every single work, an unequivocal indication of a growing disregard for the *Opera and Drama* principles.

Coupled with this new duet technique is a tendency to revert to formal musical phrases without concern for the words to which the melodic design is set. A beginning of this was noted in *Siegfried* (see p. 126). It plays a larger part in *Tristan* and an even greater role in *The Mastersingers*. Its effect is to draw the attention of the listener to the beauty of the melodic phrase, to the neglect of the conceptual, as in the following example:

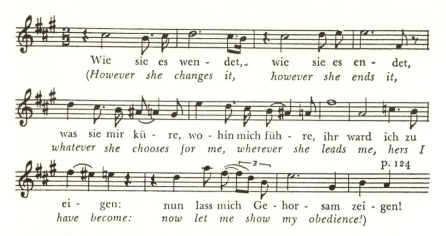

Wie sie es wen - det,_ wie sie es en - det,
(*However she changes it, however she ends it,*

was sie mir kü - re, wo - hin mich füh - re, ihr ward ich zu
whatever she chooses for me, wherever she leads me, hers I

ei - gen: nun lass mich Ge - hor - sam zei - gen!
have become: now let me show my obedience!)

p. 124

and in numerous others throughout the work.

Climaxes, both orchestral and vocal, in Acts II and III are frequently built on sequences, usually ascending and moving rapidly. Words are submerged whenever this happens. The example on page 142 illustrates the end of the long sequence pattern of the love duet from Act II.

The orchestra follows the same pattern we have traced in the verse and in the melodic line. As the medium of harmonic elucidation, it fulfills its function in Act I in a manner which sometimes, to be sure, threatens to overbalance the melodic verse but at no time disregards the spirit of the principle of subordination to the musical-poetic verse. Even at most climaxes the orchestra is quite definitely held in check. During some of them, it plays almost no role at all, as in Tristan's oath, where it supplies only tremolo background, except for the Death motif at the end.

In the other acts, the situation changes radically. In Act III, particularly during Tristan's visions, the orchestra is sustained at a more brilliant pitch for a longer time than in any other scene involving vocal music in all of Wagner's works. The texture is so rich, the tone color is so resplendent, the rhythm is so strongly accentuated, that the voice frequently is well-nigh lost in the tonal and harmonic mass of sound. The third act is the climax of the struggle, so to speak, between voice and orchestra. The tendency first noted in *Siegfried* has developed to such a degree that by sheer tonal weight the orchestral mass submerges the voice.

Motifs of reminiscence, which, as we have noted, Wagner made use of less and less in each succeeding *Ring* drama, disappear almost entirely in *Tristan*. It is clear that he is no longer concerned with relating specific past actions to subsequent action, except in the one instance of the Death motif, but now conceives of leitmotifs as orchestral themes to be treated musically as part of a symphonic web. The composer himself throws significant light on the independence and musical self-sufficiency of the leitmotifs in *Tristan and Isolde* when he speaks of the motifs in the orchestra during the third act as "restlessly emerging, developing, combining, separating, then again reuniting, growing, diminishing, finally clashing, embracing and well-nigh engulfing one another," and points out that, for their fullest expression, they require "most complete harmonization, as well as a most independent orchestral treatment." (W.S., VIII, 186)

The approximately thirty motifs which occur in *Tristan* are so thoroughly musical and symphonic in character that it is not only irrelevant, but virtually impossible, to give them accurate names. There is even considerable uncertainty about which are new motifs and which are variations of ones already stated, because of the fact that almost all are in some way or other variations of the one or two fundamental motifs announced in the opening measures of the prelude.

As a consequence, the designations of the majority of the motifs given by interpreters who regard these motifs in essentially the same light as those of the early *Ring* dramas are obscure and contradictory. In spite of their valiant efforts, the connotation even of the principal motif of the drama is quite uncertain:

It is divided into two parts, the ascending chromatic figure of measures three and four occurring well over a hundred times throughout the work. Lavignac refers to A as "the Confession," and B as "Desire." Kobbé calls A "Tristan," and B "Isolde," and the two together "the Love Potion," appending the following interesting explanation: "The first part, with its descending chro-matics, is pervaded by a certain triste mood as if Tristan were still vaguely forewarned by his conscience of the impending tragedy. The second soars ecstatically upward. It is the woman yielding unquestionably to the rapture of requited love." (*Wagner's Music Dramas Analyzed with the Leading Motives*, p. 110) Kufferath designates A as "Tristan's Suffering," B as "Desire," and the combination of the two as "Desire, or Philtre." Terry refers only to the combined motif and calls it "Love." Newman calls A "Grief" or "Sorrow," and B "Isolde's Magic," and says, "Number One will be referred to in the following analysis as the Grief or Sorrow motive, though it must be understood that its expression is too complex to be tied down to one descriptive word: it has in it something of pain, something of resignation, something of hope-lessness, and much more." (S.G.O., 100)

Furthermore, all the motifs undergo such a wide variety of changes in mood and atmosphere throughout the drama that they cannot reflect any specific mood for very long. Two motifs from the prelude to Act II are designated as "Ecstasy" and "Ardor," and a motif from later in the act as "Felicity." Certain variations of the Ardor motif become more ecstatic than the Ecstasy motif; certain variations of the Ecstasy motif are as calm and serene as the Felicity motif, which in turn, especially during Act III, works itself up to a frenzied pitch to express the height of Tristan's delirium. It is manifestly absurd to attempt to give such abstract designations to these motifs. Ernst Kurth, in his important *Romantische Har-monik und ihre Krise in Wagners "Tristan,"* discusses (pp. 502 ff.) a motif, first appearing in the sixteenth and seventeenth measures of the prelude, which, along with that of the opening measures, is the most frequently appearing leitmotif in the entire work, although not even recognized as one by the various guides and commentaries.

This indefiniteness is the most unequivocal evidence that Wagner no longer is influenced by the motif of reminiscence of *Opera and Drama*. For in that essay he wrote, "When purely musical themes were christened 'thoughts,' this was either a thoughtless misuse of the word or an example of the self-deception of the musician, who gave the name of thought to a theme, in connection with which, to be sure, he had thought something, but something which no-one else would understand, except perhaps someone to whom he had imparted in sober words what he had been thinking of. . . . A musical motif can . . . produce a definite impression only when the feeling expressed in the motif is imparted as something definite before our eyes by a definite individual in connection with a definite object. The absence of these conditions presents a musical motif to the emotions as something indefinite, and . . . no matter how often it recurs in the same form, it remains for us only the recurrence of something indefinite." (W.S., IV, 184f.)

As for the requirement that the motif be expressed "before our eyes by a definite individual," that is fulfilled in *Tristan* by only one, the Death motif. As a consequence, it alone, among them all, carries with it, on each repetition, a definite reminiscence of the original words of which it was the musical counterpart and can be referred to as a motif of reminiscence. It is effectively used with this connotation numerous times throughout the drama. One such is illustrated in the example on page 138.

This entirely different leitmotif method contributes significantly to the dominance of the music and is a major factor in making the music relatively independent of the words. It is this newly won freedom of musical expression which makes possible in *Tristan and Isolde* and all the later works the unprecedented brilliance of tonal development which was impossible under the *Opera and Drama* principles governing the synthesis.

chapter fourteen

Music of the Future

EVER SINCE the publication of *The Art-Work of the Future,* Wagner's music had been derisively labelled *Zukunfts-musik* ("music of the future") in certain circles. Wagner became more and more annoyed at this term, as we see in numerous letters and public statements, and took the opportunity in 1861 to set the record straight, or so he hoped. He did this in a typically Wagnerian preface of some fifty pages to a French prose transla-tion of *The Flying Dutchman, Tannhäuser, Lohengrin,* and *Tristan and Isolde.* This preface he entitled "Music of the Future," but the title is meant ironically. He hoped to dispel all the error and prejudice which second-hand reports about his theories had spread by an accurate restatement of those ideas.

But his new Schopenhauerian position caused complications which are at once interesting and important for our discussion of synthesis. His style seems to have been favorably influenced by the lucidity of Schopenhauer's expository prose, and the tone of the whole essay is more moderate, less polemic and dogmatic. How-ever, what Wagner intended as a restatement of the *Opera and Drama* argument reveals itself on closer study to be a tentative at-tempt to realign the elements of the *Gesamtkunstwerk* in a man-ner compatible with Schopenhauer's view of music. There is no evidence that Wagner was aware of this shift; indeed, as we shall see, he seems to be of the opinion that his theoretical position, as well as his artistic production, is still fully compatible with the theory of *Opera and Drama.* But it is easy to prove the inaccuracy of this by an analysis of the essay.

Such inconsistency might prove to be embarrassing to the Wagner scholar—It hasn't been so in the present instance, because it has never been pointed out!—except for the fact, which we hope to have long since proved, that Wagner was no original theorist. His artistic intuition guided him more surely than his dubious dialectics ever could have, and there is no serious stigma attached to an artist's not fully comprehending in philosophical and theoretical terms the directions in which his artistic nature was moving. "Music of the Future" is a revealing theoretical counterpart of *Tristan and Isolde,* which he had finished just one year earlier, and throws an interesting light on the intuitive side of Wagner's esthetics during the period of its composition. But is there any doubt which is the more important product?

Wagner's chief battle on the philosophical front had to be fought against Schopenhauer's categorical rejection of the idea of any genuine synthesis of music with the other arts. There are many passages in Schopenhauer which read like a direct contradiction to the whole basis of Wagner's work: "Grand opera is the creation, not of a pure artistic sense, but of the somewhat barbaric notion that esthetic enjoyment can be heightened by amassing the means, by the simultaneity of totally distinct varieties of impression; and that the effect can be strengthened by an increase in the total mass." Instead of being able to devote itself to the music alone, "the mind is acted upon during such highly complex opera music, simultaneously through the eye by the most colorful spectacle, the most fantastic scenes, and the most animated impressions of light and color; and at the same time the plot of the work occupies it. The mind is diverted, distracted, stupefied by all this and is thus made unreceptive to the sacred, mysterious, intense language of tones. Thus such products work directly against the attainment of the musical purpose." (A.S., V, 457) "The text of an opera should never leave a subordinate position, in order to make itself the chief element and the music a mere means of expressing it. This is a great mistake and an awful absurdity. For everywhere music expresses only the quintessence of life and its events, never these in themselves . . . therefore when music joins too closely to words and seeks to mold itself to events, it is attempting to speak a language which is not its own." (A.S., I, 345)

Of course, Wagner could not go so far in his discipleship of Schopenhauer as to accept such conclusions. While he welcomed the idea of the uniqueness of music, he had perforce to defend the legitimacy of his art synthesis. And so, using as a point of departure Schopenhauer's view of music as a revelation of the inner world, independent of the laws of causality and logic, Wagner constructed in "Music of the Future" an ingenious argument for his musical drama. Music, he says, is capable of revelations greater than those of any other art, because, it operates in an inner realm beyond the laws of logic and causality. The human, bound by these laws, is easily confused when confronted with the supra-logical revelations of music. In this the dramatic poet, if he works hand in hand with the musician, can be the mediator. The sympathetic emotion of the listener can be so profoundly affected by the drama that he is transported into an ecstatic state wherein he is in a receptive condition for the supra-logical revelations of the music.

In tracing the steps leading to this conclusion, we shall see that they are in significant ways incompatible with the opinions of *Opera and Drama*. Although Wagner intended "Music of the Future" to be a shortened restatement of his arguments and conclusions in the works of the 1849–1851 period, the summaries are actually a very inaccurate reflection of the original. Wagner gives us an unwitting confirmation of their inaccuracies by stating in the early pages of his essay that he is writing the summaries without having reread the original documents. His reason: he has not been in the proper frame of mind to review his own theories! This is a Freudian compulsion if there ever was one.

In "Music of the Future" he significantly accepts poetry and music as separate and legitimate forms of art. In *Opera and Drama* he had refused to admit their right to exist as separate entities outside a synthesis. The history of music which he outlined in that essay and in *The Art-Work of the Future* was a continuous account of the various subterfuges that composers have invented throughout the ages to attempt to compensate for the inadequacy of expression of music alone. (W.S., III, 81–101, 233–320) In "Music of the Future" his supposed summary of this discussion traces the gradual emergence of music as an independent art form. He speaks of Italian Renaissance church music, for instance, as producing "such a wonderful, intensely moving effect . . . that absolutely no other art is capable of anything comparable." (W.S., VII, 107)

In *The Art-Work of the Future* he had said, "Counterpoint is artificial art playing with itself, the mathematics of feeling, the mechanical rhythm of egoistic harmony." (W.S., III, 88) Contrapuntal harmony, he now says in "Music of the Future," produces "an absolutely unique effect of the most irresistible power." (W.S., VII, 108)

Wagner's account of the development of the symphony through Haydn, Mozart, and Beethoven is highly colored by Schopenhauer. He writes that the symphony is a direct revelation out of another world. It discloses a relationship of phenomena quite different from the logical one to which we are accustomed and thus confuses us. Though it overwhelms us emotionally, it is unable to satisfy our logical reasoning powers. (W.S., VII, 110) This is the definition of music he needs to perform his new kind of musical-dramatic synthesis.

He goes even farther astray in his ostensible account of his previous discussions on the development of poetry. In "Music of the Future" he stresses the preoccupation of great poets with the problem of the relation of drama and music. The earlier essays actually contained no such discussion. He contrasts the theoretical willingness of Voltaire, Lessing, Goethe, and Schiller to accept a combination of the two arts, with their antipathy toward opera, which was the only form in which such a combination existed. What is it, he asks, that makes the poet so intensely interested in music? In his desire to add an emotional impact to the conventional meaning of his verse, he employs rhythmic devices and the "almost musical decorative effect of rhyme." (W.S., VII, 104) (The reader will recall what Wagner had said about regular rhythm and rhyme in the earlier essays.) But the poet senses his limitations and recognizes the far greater potentiality of music for emotional appeal. It is for this reason that he seeks a union of poetry and music.

Just as the poet needs the musician, says Wagner, so also the musician needs the poet, because the revelations of music cannot be brought to the listener as long as he is still bound to the laws of causality. The listener is moved emotionally but is confused by the new values which are being revealed, and in his uncertainty he grasps for the support of those laws to which he is accustomed. He asks the question: Why? He can receive no answer from the music. The dramatic poet, aware of the capabilities of the music, must here come to the listener's aid. By casting his dramatic poem in a form in which it penetrates into the most delicate threads of the musical texture, the poet can so completely capture the emotional sympathy of the listener by the visible performance of a life-like action that the listener is transported into an ecstatic state in which he no longer feels his connection with the causal world and submits himself to the new laws which are revealed to him by the music. (W.S., VII, 112)

It is clear that this theory replaces the three-fold union of poetry, visual action and music of *Opera and Drama* with a new dual synthesis of drama and music. It is equally evident that the role of music in this synthesis is a more independent one. Nevertheless, Wagner, not conscious of any such basic alteration in the elements of his synthesis, goes on to explain that the technique of uniting the verse with the music was to be as outlined in *Opera and Drama*. (W.S., VII, 112) The principles of modulation, harmonic elucidation by the orchestra, coincidence of verse and speech accent, musical and poetic alliteration (to which has been added rhyme), musical underlining of gesture, and motifs of reminiscence he still assumed to be valid. But with the change in emphasis in favor of music, a modification in the application of these principles and a relaxation of the rigidity with which music was coordinated with the verse and action were inevitable. We have seen that this is exactly what took place in *Tristan and Isolde*.

This loosening of the controls, so to speak, is implicit in the course of the remainder of the essay, in which Wagner goes on to assert that neither the musician nor the poet need sacrifice any of his powers to this union. Quite to the contrary, he states, both will feel more unconstrained. For without the collaboration of poetry, the musician would hesitate to give free rein to the limitless possibilities of musical expression for fear of awakening the impulse in the listener to ask, Why? Such union gives him the necessary link with the phenomenal world which makes this restraint superfluous. And the poet who is aware of the limitless expressive potentialities of the music will consciously strive to fit his poem to the fine nuances of the music. In so doing, he will perceive a greatly widened scope of emotional appeal, and his awareness of this will make it possible for him to draft the poetic conception with boundless freedom. The poet will say to the musician, "Plunge fearlessly into the full tide of the sea of music; hand in hand with me you can never lose touch with what is most comprehensible to everyone; for because of me you stand on the solid ground of the dramatic action, and that action at the moment of its presentation on the stage is the most directly understandable of all poems. Expand your melody boldly so that it pours like a ceaseless stream over the entire work: in it say what I refrain from saying because only you can say it, and silently I will utter everything because it is my hand that guides you." (W.S., VII, 129) When one thinks of the relationship which obtained in *Opera and Drama*, it is evident from this quotation that the mutual freedom from restraint is more significant for the music than for the poetry.

"Music of the Future" is the essay in which Wagner makes the famous remark, so often incautiously cited by Wagner scholars, about *Tristan and Isolde:* "I will allow the strictest demands growing out of my theoretical assertions to be made of this work." (W.S., VII, 119) When considered in the light of the theory, it can be seen that its implications are quite different from what they seem when used out of context. *Tristan* should be considered as the creative parallel to the point of view expressed in "Music of the Future," which we have seen to be a quite different one from *Opera and Drama*. It is a major error to use this statement as ex post facto proof that in *Tristan* the principles of *Opera and Drama* were in full force. Any possible doubt as to the true state of affairs is dispelled by the continuation of this remark. Wagner goes on to say, ". . . not because I shaped it according to my system, for I had completely forgotten all theory; but because here at last I moved with the utmost freedom and with utter disregard of any theoretical scruple, to such an extent that while I wrote I had the sense of far surpassing my system. Believe me, there is no greater satisfaction for the artist than this feeling of total lack of reflection which I experienced in writing my *Tristan*." (W.S., VII, 119)

"Music of the Future" is Wagner's first attempt to use metaphysics to justify his ideal drama. We have seen that it was a tentative one. Two further essays, *Beethoven* and *The Destiny of Opera*, make out of the unconscious impulse a deliberate process and recast the theory of the *Gesamtkunstwerk* into metaphysical terms derived from Schopenhauer.

chapter fifteen

Beethoven

IT SEEMS BEST to disregard chronology at this point and finish the discussion of theory with the essays *Beethoven* (1870) and *The Destiny of Opera* (1871). This postpones consideration of *The Mastersingers,* which was completed in 1867. But there is considerable advantage to be gained by doing this. The essays are Wagner's definitive solution to the problems which caused inconsistencies in his "Music of the Future," and they offer the best, indeed the only adequate, framework for understanding *The Mastersingers* and the later works.

Wagner published *Beethoven* in 1870 as a contribution to the centennial of the composer's birth. It gives a full-length portrait of Beethoven as Wagner saw him, and some discerning analyses of his works, particularly the symphonies and the late quartets. But more important for us, it contains what amounts to a new theory of the synthesis of the arts, a theory which succeeds, in Wagner's eyes at least, in justifying a *Gesamtkunstwerk* in terms of Schopenhauer's theories on art, which ruled out synthesis in no uncertain terms. In its most essential form, the new theoretical *Gesamtkunstwerk* is a synthesis of music and visual action as complementary revelations, or objectifications, of the metaphysical will. In this dualistic synthesis, dialog—that which in the new synthesis corresponds to the melodic verse of *Opera and Drama*—is relegated to a subordinate position, as a mechanical aid to clarifying the mimetic action. Such a synthesis of poetic verse and vocal line as formed the very core of the earlier theory is declared an impossibility. How else could the following quotation be interpreted? "Through the experience that a piece of music loses nothing of its character when even the most diverse texts are set to it [this he has taken directly from Schopenhauer], it becomes clear that the relation of music to poetry is a sheer illusion: for it can be confirmed that when words are sung to music, it is not the poetic thought which is comprehended . . . but at most the mood it engendered in the musician as music and to music. A union of music and poetry must therefore constantly result in such a subordination of the latter that it is only surprising to see how our great German poets have again and again pondered and even attempted a union of the two arts." (W.S., IX, 103–04) The importance of this new relationship between word and music is fundamental. For if text and music stand in such an unequal association with one another, then all of the many details involving prosody and voice leading, poetic and melodic alliteration, modulation, motifs of reminiscence, etc., in other words, most of the practical esthetic details in *Opera and Drama* can no longer be valid either.

Such matters are not discussed at all in *Beethoven,* which is concerned only with the metaphysical justification of the synthesis of visual drama and music. The new *Gesamtkunstwerk* is established only on broad philosophical lines. There is none of the concrete detail and practical suggestion which were so abundant in *Opera and Drama.* This is undoubtedly one of the reasons why *Beethoven* has not received the attention it deserves in this connection. One error begets another. Because *Beethoven* has been largely disregarded, the theories it embodies have been allowed little importance in Wagner study. Because the theories of *Beethoven* have not been considered important, those of *Opera and Drama* have been accepted as the ultimate statement of Wagner's esthetics. And, finally, because the validity of *Opera and Drama* has been extended throughout Wagner's entire mature period, analyses of the music dramas have always used it to explain Wagner's theoretical position. This gives us a dangerously distorted picture of his intentions in the works from *Siegfried* on, and urgently needs correcting.

In a diary entry dated December 8, 1858, Wagner wrote that he was contemplating a "correction of certain of his [Schopenhauer's] imperfections. . . . The subject becomes more interesting to me daily, because it is a question here of conclusions which

I am the only person able to draw, because there never has been a man who was poet and musician at the same time as I am and to whom therefore insights into inner processes were possible such as are not to be expected from anyone else." (M.W., 81) Bearing in mind that Wagner's chief aim in *Beethoven* was to justify a *Gesamtkunstwerk* constructed upon Schopenhauer's theories, which admitted of none, let us examine his argument.

Schopenhauer, while asserting that music was a direct objectification of the real essence of the universe, which he further identified as the will, believed that it was impossible to communicate this will to our consciousness in terms of the phenomenal world. He held his conception of the unique character of music to be therefore essentially unprovable, "because it assumes a relationship of music as [Platonic] Idea to that which by its nature can never be Idea [i.e., the metaphysical will] and makes music the copy of an original which can itself never be directly presented as Idea." (A.S., 339) It is Wagner's contention in *Beethoven* that proof of this *is* possible, and that a demonstration of its possibility existed in the very theories of Schopenhauer, whose insufficient knowledge of music alone prevented him from recognizing this fact. (W.S., IX, 66) And so, by drawing selectively on Schopenhauer's own theories, Wagner develops his ideal drama, a dramatic music in organic connection with dramatic action, as one in which the metaphysical will is transmitted to our consciousness.

In *The World as Will and Idea* Schopenhauer had written, "All possible efforts, excitements, and manifestations of the will, all those processes within man which reason includes in the broad negative concept of feeling, may be expressed by the infinite number of possible melodies, but always in the universal, in the pure form, without the material, always according to the thing-in-itself, not the phenomenon; the innermost soul, as it were, of the phenomenon, without the body. This intense relationship which music has to the true essence of all things also explains the fact that whenever suitable music is played to any scene, action, event, or surroundings, the music seems to disclose to us its most secret meaning and appears to be the most accurate and distinct commentary upon it." (A.S., I, 345–46) Using this principle as a point of departure, Wagner declares that the inner laws of music are

also the inner laws by which drama is constructed. He considers
an intuitive awareness of this fact an a priori qualification for the
dramatist, just as the unconscious awareness of the laws of causality is the a priori qualification for perception of the world of
phenomena. (W.S., IX, 105f.) "Music . . . *includes* the drama
within itself, since the drama itself expresses the only Idea of the
world adequate to music. Drama towers over the limitations of
poetry in the same way that music towers over those of every other
art, its effect lying in the realm of the sublime. Just as drama does
not depict human characters, but lets them display themselves
directly, so music gives us in its motifs the character of all phenomena of the world according to their innermost essence. Not
only are the movement, configuration and evolution of these
motifs analogous solely to the drama, but the drama representing
the Idea can in truth be completely understood only through
those moving and evolving musical motifs. We would then not
be in error if we saw in music the a priori qualification for fashioning a drama. As we construct the phenomenal world by application
of the laws of time and space which exist a priori in our brain, so
this conscious presentation of the Idea of the world in the drama
would be conditioned by the inner laws of music, which assert
themselves in the dramatist unconsciously much as we draw on the
laws of causality in our perception of the phenomenal world."
(W.S., IX, 105)

Wagner asserts that a dim awareness of this fact accounts for
the preoccupation of poets with the relationship between poetry
and music. Because of it, too, the inexplicable genius of Shakespeare can be best understood by a study of his only peer among
musicians, Beethoven. "If we take the total impression of Shakespeare's world of shapes with the exceptional pithiness of every
character moving in it and hold up to this the sum total of Beethoven's world of motifs with its ineluctable incisiveness and precision, we become aware that one of these worlds covers the other
so completely that each is contained in the other, even though they
seem to move in completely different spheres." (W.S., IX, 107)

Shakespeare and Beethoven are alike, he continues, in that
their creations are subject to the laws governing each particular
form of art, while at the same time transcending those laws to such

an extent that the latter no longer seem to exist. (W.S., IX, 108) Therefore, Wagner maintains, the most consummate art form would be that which united the two at the point where their individual spheres touch. The transitional point of these two spheres can best be illustrated, he says, by an analogy with Schopenhauer's theory of dreams, clairvoyance, and apparitions.

In Volume I of *Parerga and Paralipomena* Wagner found a rather long essay entitled "On the Seeing of Spirits and Related Matters," which he now used as a kind of catalytic agent to unite Schopenhauer's metaphysics of music with his own conception of the *Gesamtkunstwerk*. Although Schopenhauer's essay has nothing to do with his theory of art, he reveals his belief in the transcendental nature of dreams and clairvoyance in numerous passages throughout *The World as Will and Idea*. To relate this to art, which for the Romantics was also revelatory, could not have seemed as strange to Wagner's audience as we may find it now.

In this essay Schopenhauer attempts an idealistic explanation of clairvoyance and the phenomenon of dreams. According to him, since perception is basically intellectual and not sensory, a function of the brain and not of the senses, which only stimulate the brain to action, it is perfectly possible for some extrasensory force also to cause the brain to function. Because this force is usually at work during sleep, whether normal or clairvoyant, Schopenhauer calls it the dream organ. (A.S., IV, 272) Ordinary dreams are the result of the action of the dream organ, but its strongest excitation results in clairvoyance, where direct contact is made with the metaphysical will. Dreams in deep sleep are of this same nature. But these clairvoyant visions or revelatory dreams are not transmissible as such to our consciousness, since the latter is bound to phenomenal laws. Therefore, says Schopenhauer, they are sometimes interpreted by the brain just before we awaken, in what he terms an allegorical dream, which approaches the phenomenal world closely enough to be perceived by our conscious self. (A.S., IV, 289–90) These are the prophetic dreams which, he says, have been reported by trustworthy sources in all periods of history and from all parts of the civilized world.

Music, says Wagner, can be compared with this allegorical dream, since it likewise is a revelation of the will in terms which are perceptible to our waking consciousness. For, just as the allegorical dream is an intermediate step between clairvoyance and wakefulness, approaching the phenomenal world sufficiently to perform its function of transmitting the will, but not coinciding with it, so music establishes contact with the conceptual world, while not coinciding with it as the other arts do. Whereas all other forms of art deal with phenomena, music alone is not bound to the phenomenal world and is a direct objectification of the will. Through rhythm, however, music is related to the laws of time, and since rhythm is derived originally from the dance, to the laws of space as well. Thus music, like the allegorical dream, has a partial connection with the conceptual world; hence the validity of the analogy. (W.S., IX, 172–77)

Wagner establishes the contact between visual drama and the will by relating it to the perception of apparitions, which Schopenhauer considers analogous to clairvoyance. According to Schopenhauer's hypothesis, while the body is in a state of partial wakefulness, the dream organ projects its visions into the brain at the same time as the brain is registering external phenomena through the mediation of the senses. But this dual stimulation interferes with the normal sensory stimulus, and the effect of the latter is not as strong as usual. The inner vision, called forth by the dream organ, is superimposed upon the vaguely discerned phenomenal surroundings, and the result is an apparition or vision. (A.S., IV, 309–11)

The apparition or vision Wagner compares with drama, which is likewise an intermediate revelation of the inner clairvoyant vision of the poet, expressed in terms of time and space and projected into the surrounding of the waking consciousness, while the senses, particularly the sense of sight, are in a partial state of depotentiation. (W.S., IX, 108) This depotentiation of the senses, which is a necessary postulate for the perception of the vision, is accomplished for the drama by music. Wagner here refers to the effect which music has on a sympathetic listener in a concert hall. One who is absorbed in the music, with his eyes wide open, sees none of the distracting sights upon which his eyes are resting. (W.S., IX, 75)

Now, when the composer and the dramatist are one and the same person, his clairvoyant vision of the essence of the universe is the single impulse which is simultaneously transmitted to us in two complementary ways, in terms of visual drama and in terms of music. Each is therefore in its own way an expression of the same clairvoyant vision of the metaphysical will. (W.S., IX, 109–11)

It is necessarily implicit in this new system that the component elements of the synthesis bear a different relation to one another than in the earlier theories. We have seen that the original equality and interdependence of the three phases of drama—visual action, poetry, and music—as expressed in *Opera and Drama*, had to be adjusted in "Music of the Future" to accommodate a new conception in which the music was admittedly the most powerful medium for the communication of the artistic impulse. Poetry and visual action were to provide a kind of cathartic experience which was necessary to prepare the listener for the revelations embodied in the music. Thus, poetic verse and visual action each played a role of equal importance, while the music was in a class apart.

In *Beethoven* the visual action is raised to a level almost equal to the music, and the organic word-tone relationship, which in "Music of the Future" had been retained at least nominally, is dissolved, the poetry playing a minor role altogether subordinate to the other two. This is very pointedly expressed in *Beethoven*, when Wagner says that "music loses none of its character even when very different kinds of texts are set to it," and concludes that "the relationship of music to poetry is a thoroughly illusory one." (W.S., IX, 103) This shows vividly how far Wagner had departed from his opinions in *Opera and Drama*. For in the earlier work, he had used precisely this idea to show the *incorrect* relation between absolute melody and poetic verse which had existed until his time in opera: "The melody, which remained conscious of its ability for infinite emotional expression acquired by virtue of its being in music's own domain, paid no attention at all to the sensuous setting of the verse, since the latter could only seriously impede music in its use of its own resources. It rather proclaimed itself as independent vocal melody in an expressive manner which rendered the emotional content of the verse in only the most general way, and in a specifically musical setting, to which the verse was like a mere explanatory label placed beneath a painting." (W.S., IV, 113)

The final movement of Beethoven's *Ninth Symphony* serves here once again to illustrate the wide difference between Wagner's conception of the relationship between poetry and music in this essay and in his *Opera and Drama*. In both essays, it is this movement which Wagner considered the immediate forerunner of his ideal drama. But in the earlier period, it was the organic relationship between words and music that represented the decisive step toward the ideal drama. In *Beethoven* the significance of this same movement is not related to its poetic content. "We know that it is not the verse of the poet, be it even Goethe's or Schiller's, which can determine the music," he writes now. In *The Art-Work of the Future* he had written, "The living flesh of tone is the human voice. The word is bone and muscle of the human voice. In the decisiveness of the word the ever moving emotion, which overflowed into the art of tone, finds its sure, unerring expression, by means of which it can comprehend and clearly express itself. Thus it gains its most exalted satisfaction as well as its most satisfying exaltation through tone become speech in music become poetry." (W.S., III, 74) In *Beethoven*, Wagner writes that the final movement of the *Ninth* "is a cantata with text, to which the music is related no more closely than to any other song text." (W.S., IX, 111) The crucial step is now represented as the transition from instrumental to vocal music, the union of voice and orchestra marking the beginning of the transition from orchestral music to the ideal drama. The only thing, he says, which can condition music is the drama. He makes clear that he means by this, not the dramatic poem, but the "drama actually taking place before our eyes as a visible image of the music, where the word and the dialog belong solely to the action, not to the poetic thought." (W.S., IX, 112) Thus, instead of the musical-poetic verse being the "life-giving center" of the synthesis, the sole determining agent for the music in the ideal drama is the dramatic action.

This dualistic concept of the musical drama has a distinct similarity with Nietzsche's *The Birth of Tragedy Out of the Spirit of Music* and it is indeed likely that Nietzsche had some influence in its development. *The Birth of Tragedy* appeared in 1872, with a dedication to Wagner, two years after Wagner's essay, but the two men had met in 1868 (when Nietzsche was twenty-four and Wagner fifty-five), and for a number of years Nietzsche was a frequent visitor at Tribschen. It was during these years, as T. M. Campbell has shown (see bibliography), that the essential ideas of *The Birth of Tragedy* were being developed, and it is on record that these matters were discussed together by the two men, whose mutual interest in Schopenhauer was a strong bond between them. Kurt Hildebrandt points out (see bibliography) that Nietzsche had read an earlier essay, "The Dionysian View of Life," a preliminary form of *The Birth of Tragedy,* to Wagner. Yet, as he goes on to state, the influences exerted by the two men were reciprocal and an accurate picture of the contribution of each to the theories of the other is not possible. More recently Curt von Westernhagen in *Richard Wagner, sein Werk, sein Wesen, seine Welt* makes the claim that the germ idea of Nietzsche's *The Birth of Tragedy* came from Wagner, but he fails to support this view with convincing evidence.

chapter sixteen

The Destiny of Opera

THE DESTINY OF OPERA (1871) is, in a sense, a continuation of the Beethoven essay, for it is the elaboration of an idea expressed in the earlier work, where Wagner had written, "The most perfect form of art . . . is that wherein all vestiges of conventionality are completely removed from the drama as well as from the music." (W.S., IX, 112) The form of this idea as developed in *The Destiny of Opera* defines the ideal drama as a "mimetic-musical improvisation of consummate poetic value fixed by the finest artistic judgment." (W.S., IX, 149)

The destiny of opera (by "opera" he of course means his own synthesis) is nothing less than the regeneration of the German theater, which Wagner considered to be in a most dismal state. In this essay, written as a thesis following his election as a member of the Royal Academy of Arts in Berlin, he notes the popularity of traditional opera and asks why it should command more respect and attention than the drama, in spite of its triviality. The fault lies, he says, in drama itself and in "the impossibility, within its limits and with the expressive powers at its disposal, of satisfying the demands of the ideal drama." (W.S., IX, 134) Dramatic poets have been at a loss to explain the intensity with which their emotions were acted upon by performances of Mozart and Gluck. They were forced to admit that the music transported them immediately into the very sphere of ideality which they were vainly hoping to reach in their own way. For by means of the music the simplest feature of the action was exalted. There was no need for philosophic truths, with which the poets had felt that they must fill out their dramas, for the innermost essence of the wisest sentence was directly revealed by pertinent melodic crystallization. The most lofty pathos was the very soul of these works. (W.S., IX, 139)

What confounded the poets in this discovery, says Wagner, was their understandable reluctance to concede such significance to an art form in which the music so dominated the drama and to which the poet contributed so little. The resolution of the dilemma, he says, is a union of drama and music in which each is enabled to develop its own powers unimpeded by the other. This is of course the Wagnerian synthesis.

Dealing first with the dramatic aspect, he argues that the strength of great dramatists, Lope de Vega, Molière, Aeschylus, and especially Shakespeare, lay in their intimate knowledge of the theater. All had a genuine comprehension of their medium, all understood the force and impact of good "theater," and all raised the level of the theatrical art of their day. In their function as dramatists, they felt themselves to be actors as well as poets. As a consequence, the works they produced were so eminently actable that in their mimetic naturalness they resembled improvised performances such as those of the *commedia dell' arte,* which played so important a part in the early development of the modern theater. The roles felt so right to the actors, every speech or action called for showed such an intimate understanding of the actors' problems, that the actors were able to lose themselves as easily as though they were improvising. But because the dramatists possessed creative genius, they were able to infuse into those "fixed improvisations" a poetic quality which raised them to a high esthetic level without sacrificing mimetic naturalness. These eminently playable dramatic works, theatrical in the best sense, of high esthetic quality, Wagner defines for his purposes as "fixed mimetic improvisations of consummate poetic value." (W.S., IX, 143)

It is this spirit which, according to Wagner, is lacking in modern drama and which needs to be returned to the drama to make possible the revitalization of the theater. Among modern writers for the stage he finds the sure sense of theater and miming only in the otherwise unworthy efforts of such mediocrities as Iffland and Kotzebue. Not without some malice, he offers Hebbel to illustrate what happens when a gifted literary figure who lacks theatrical experience attempts to write dramas "to illustrate philo-

sophical theses." The fact that Hebbel had published a Nibelungen trilogy in 1862, while Wagner was still at work on his own,
had caused him no pleasure. He holds that work up to ridicule in
his next essay, *Actors and Singers.*

"The actual stage play," says Wagner, "in the most modern
sense of the word would surely have to be the basis for all future
dramatic efforts." (W.S., IX, 151–52) It is clear from this statement
that he was not trying to fool himself or anybody else by his
paradoxical and provocative term "fixed improvisation." He meant
the kind of good, playable stage work that an old hand at theater
production could turn out on the strength of his intimate ac-
quaintance with the theater, independent of any formal literary
tradition. His full definition adds the permanent literary value of
dramatic geniuses like Shakespeare, Lope de Vega, and Molière
(not to forget Wagner himself).

Since Wagner is really more interested in this essay in re-
defining his concept of the *Gesamtkunstwerk* than he is in initi-
ating a revitalization of the German stage, he is not satisfied with
laying the theoretical foundation for the regeneration of the spoken
drama. This fixed mimetic improvisation must be paralleled by a
fixed musical improvisation, and Wagner moves into the musical
sphere with the contention that drama can reach its loftiest height
and its ideal form only when the poetical visualization of a dramatic action is synthesized with simultaneous musical realization.
"If every action, each most ordinary incident of life, when reproduced as mimic play reveals itself to us in the transfiguring light
and with the objective effect of a mirror image, . . . we must
observe that this image reveals itself in the transfiguration of purest
ideality when it is dipped in the magic spring of music and is
presented to us as pure form, so to speak, freed from any realistic
materiality." (W.S., IX, 146)

Having used Shakespeare as the alter ego of his own dramatic
sense, he now again turns to Beethoven as his musical alter ego,
as he did in his preceding essay. "Earwitness" accounts, he says,
testify to the extraordinary improvisational powers of Beethoven;
they were so remarkable it is to be regretted that they could not
have been written down and preserved. Had that been possible,
they might well have been even greater than the works which we

do possess. Wagner claims this by analogy with the supposed superiority of the improvisations by mediocre composers to their written compositions. This dubious point in his otherwise ingenious argument could have been strengthened if Wagner had only placed more stress on the improvisational character of many of Beethoven's published works. It is an easily demonstrable contention that Beethoven in his late period constantly felt impelled to overstep the bounds of the forms in which he was writing. Liszt, in a letter to Wilhelm von Lenz, congratulating him on his biography of Beethoven, divided his works "very logically into two categories: one in which the traditional and conventional form contains and rules thought, and the other in which thought recreates and fashions form and style at the behest of its needs and its inspiration." (L.F.L., I, 152) The C-sharp minor quartet, opus 131, for example, is in large part so independent of formal patterns that it approaches very closely what Wagner meant by fixed improvisation.

Wagner argues the possibility of releasing musical composition completely from arbitrary formal patterns by combining it with stage action, or more specifically, with his fixed mimetic improvisation, thus permitting it a freedom of expression subject only to the unique formal requirements which grow from within the music itself. By releasing music from externally imposed formal strictures, a kind of free improvisation is effected. However, just as in the drama, this improvisation can be fixed on a high artistic level by the musical genius of a great composer. The result is fixed musical improvisation. It can be seen at once that this concept is a more original one than the fixed mimetic improvisation; whereas the latter is basically a restatement of the idea underlying the term "stage play," fixed musical improvisation is a significant new pattern for musical composition in a large-scale work and a more considerable contribution to the theory of the *Gesamtkunstwerk*.

Wagner is now ready for the final step, the combination of fixed mimetic and fixed musical improvisation into a single work. This synthesis yields the full definition already quoted, with which the argument of the essay culminates: a mimetic-musical improvisation of consummate poetic value fixed by the finest artistic judgment. The definition becomes the more plausible when one reflects that Wagner is really speaking, not of Shakespeare and Beethoven, nor of a poet and a composer, but of himself, the dramatist-composer in one, in whose consciousness the two aspects are inextricably interwoven.

Thus, *The Destiny of Opera* is a kind of corollary to the earlier, more important *Beethoven*. It is Wagner's last formal discussion of synthesis. But statements scattered throughout the other essays and articles of his last period indicate that he continued to think of his ideal drama in these terms. "I would almost like to call my dramas acts of music become visible." "The music sounds, and what it sounds you may see on the stage before you." "The drama [is] the visible image of music." Such expressions are all restatements of the thesis of the two essays. In both theories, the music and the dramatic action are parallel but essentially independent of one another. The music expresses in its way what is also presented in visual terms on the stage. Only the most general agreement is postulated. The relationship is an ideal one, within which each enjoys a high degree of freedom. Thus the fixed mimetic-musical improvisation is not impeded by any complex rules of interrelationship and both the singer-actor and the instrumentalist are free to follow the fixed improvisations of their writer and composer with the minimum of constraint. This is indeed a far cry from *Opera and Drama,* where the entire interrelationship among the elements of the synthesis was so painstakingly and minutely explained; but it is the theory which is the counterpart of *The Mastersingers* and the one from which that great work can best be viewed.

chapter seventeen

The Mastersingers

AS I HAVE said before, *The Mastersingers* was completed in 1867, three and four years respectively before the two essays just discussed. Though the theory trailed several years behind the work, the reverse chronology need not disturb us. There is plenty of evidence that the train of thought which ultimately yielded the theory had its origins during the *Mastersinger* period of the early and middle sixties.

Of all his music dramas, *The Mastersingers* is the actors' work par excellence, and it can be no accident that the work and the theory which both lay the greatest stress on the mime should come in such close proximity. Wagner had always been interested in acting; he wrote about it at all stages of his career. There is much evidence that he was an accomplished, if untrained, actor in his own right. Up to 1849 his theatrical experience in Würzburg, Magdeburg, Königsberg, Riga and other places, and for years in Dresden had been rich and varied. After his flight into exile in Switzerland, however, there had come a long hiatus and it was not until the early sixties that he again became actively involved with the theater. Above all, it was Ludwig's Munich and the model performances of *Tristan and Isolde* in 1865 which must have reawakened his always latent interest in acting.

This renewed contact with the stage eventually yielded on the one hand *The Mastersingers,* and on the other, the new definition of the ideal drama as a "mimetic-musical improvisation of consummate poetic value fixed by the finest artistic judgment," and this is the definition which fits the great comic drama perfectly. Any attempt to relate *The Mastersingers,* as we have the previous works, to *Opera and Drama* would result only in the demonstration that the two are incompatible. The juxtaposition of the elements of the *Gesamtkunstwerk* is wrong; the emphases are wrong; the role of the orchestra is far different from what *Opera and Drama* demanded; there are choruses, duets, a quintet; there is even a delightful ballet. It takes some energetic looking the other way to explain *The Mastersingers* in terms of *Opera and Drama*, although it has often been tried.

The Mastersingers is, on the other hand, the very embodiment of Wagner's paradoxical fixed improvisation. It is lively theater from beginning to end. The performers seem to glide through their roles with the minimum of effort and the maximum of enjoyment, and the impression is that everything is right for them. There is a feeling of improvisational freedom. There are four ostensible, but very convincing improvisations written into its plot: Walter's trial song in Act I before the mastersingers in his vain attempt to be accepted into the guild; Beckmesser's luckless serenade to Eva to the unwanted accompaniment of Hans Sachs's cobbling in Act II; the baptismal ensemble ending Scene 1 of Act III, during which five singers join in christening Walter's new song "die selige Morgentraumdeutweise"; and most important, the dream song itself, improvised by Walter according to the mastersingers' rules as explained to him in the intervals of his improvisation by Hans Sachs, and copied down (one is tempted to say "fixed") by the latter in Scene 1 of Act III.

Its recurrence as the prize song in the final scene is an extraordinary example of fixed improvisation. Beckmesser, who had stolen the song, but had been unable to memorize it in time, has sung a riotous parody of it and has been laughed off the singer's platform. In his rage and confusion, he admits publicly that he is not the author of the supposedly preposterous work, accuses Sachs of being the writer, and stalks off the stage and out of the play. Sachs hands the manuscript to the mastersingers, calling on Walter to prove his authorship and show how the song should really be sung. With the manuscript before them, the mastersingers check the first few lines as Walter sings them, but, greatly moved by the beauty of the song, in such glorious contrast to Beckmesser's travesty, they let the manuscript fall to the ground and listen without following the text. Perceiving this, Walter no longer feels limited to the original version and "improvises" a quite different version on the spot under the inspiration of the moment.

There is an emphasis on mimetic movement which is the very essence of visual theater in this, by far the most animated of all Wagner's works. Dialog is often dispensed with entirely. The opening scene is an example. In this, Walter uses the intervals between phrases of the chorale sung by the congregation to try to attract Eva's attention by gestures. More striking in its mimetic appeal to the eye is the final scene of Act I, beginning at the moment when Beckmesser storms out of the marker's enclosure in a fury over Walter's song. At the climax of this grandiose mimetic-musical spectacle, sixteen different vocal lines are running along simultaneously with the confused and colorful action. Everyone is talking at once, and we can detect only from their actions (and from the music) what they must be saying. Beckmesser is venomously and vociferously railing against the mistakes in Walter's trial song, moving down the line from one mastersinger to the other; the latter are expressing various degrees of dissatisfaction with Walter; the apprentices, overstimulated by the confusion, are singing and dancing with delight; Walter, with Sachs's encouragement, doggedly continues his trial song amid the din; while Hans Sachs himself stands apart from the others, voicing his admiration of Walter's undisciplined but inspiring poetic ability. All this goes on at the same time, and added to it is the heavy polyphonic texture of the orchestra; a veritable realization of Wagner's improvisation theory.

The second act contains the broadly comic serenade of Beckmesser, punctuated at first with interruptions by Hans Sachs, who loudly and lustily sings a cobbler's ditty, ostensibly unaware of Beckmesser's proximity, but in reality knowing full well what he is doing. Later, the ill-fated serenade is devastatingly riddled by blows from Sachs's hammer; Beckmesser has let himself be maneuvered into agreeing to have Sachs record infractions of the mastersingers' prosodic and melodic rules with a hammer blow on the shoes he is finishing for Beckmesser's appearance in the great contest the next day. When the latter in desperation finally resolves to ignore the noisy tallying of mistakes and sings on stubbornly, while Sachs pounds away, noting the infractions until the shoes are completely finished, there is another mimetic-musical fixed improvisation as impressive as it is irresistible. This is farce, the chief delight of the early improvisational stage, in the grand manner.

Out of it grows the amazing street riot scene, which begins when David first sees Beckmesser serenading Magdalena in Eva's window. It rapidly develops into the most violent confusion on the stage, a real brawl, a chaos of action and of musical dialog as well. Simultaneously the orchestra plays its own version of the brawl, a complex free polyphonic development of a fugal figure derived from Beckmesser's serenade.

One of the most delightful syntheses of action and music—to the total exclusion of words—is the comic interlude of Beckmesser in Sachs's house during the first scene of Act III. Here a sequence of ideas is ingeniously communicated by a synchronization of action and music. Beckmesser, battered and bruised from the beating he has received at the hands of David in the street brawl the night before, sits on Sachs's cobbler's bench but starts up again as it awakens memories of his troubles with the cobbler. This we hear in the orchestra, which plays a combination of the music associated with Sachs's cobbling plus some strains of Beckmesser's serenade. His memories begin to get the better of him and he is thrown into utter confusion by the vividness of his recollections, all this communicated to us by the development in the orchestra of the brawl music. From one idea to another, he is led to the thought that he is badly in need of a new tune for his prize song—this revealed to us by bits of his serenade in fragmentary form—when his eyes catch sight of Walter's dream song on the table. The contrast between the coldness and ridiculousness of Beckmesser's song and the warm tones of the dream song which we now hear is most thrilling. The whole scene is a most remarkable mimetic-musical sequence and a striking illustration of the improvisation theory of *The Destiny of Opera*.

As I said in the last chapter, Wagner's theory of synthesis in this essay makes the orchestra, not the musical dialog, musically dominant. The latter no longer has the central position of the musical-poetic verse of *Opera and Drama* and in the works immediately following. It is in fact now part of the mimetic action. The musical dialog in *The Mastersingers* seems to be the point where the independent spheres of dramatic action and music, which otherwise operate in their separate media according to their own needs and laws, meet effortlessly. The center of gravity, musically speaking, is in the orchestra, and it shifts to the stage only for the formal musical numbers, where the words of the dialog are of minor importance.

The idealistic spirit of this synthesis implies the converse of the precisely calculated organic relationships which were developed in *Opera and Drama*. Instead of the minute detail into which that blueprint entered for the purpose of fixing the exact reciprocal relationship of word and tone and visual action, only the most general agreement is postulated between the mimetic action and its musical equivalent. The orchestral music, as a partially phenomenal expression, in direct contact with the will, analogous to the intermediate dream of the clairvoyant, is conceived as a metaphysical parallel of the likewise only semi-phenomenal stage action, analogous to the visions perceived by the partially clairvoyant brain of the spirit-seer. The relation between orchestra and stage action is thus an ideal one which is not more exactly defined and which permits a high degree of freedom to each of the two components.

The orchestra in *The Mastersingers* is the epitome of this principle. Its texture is fuller and more continuous than in any work preceding it. For the most part, it supplies a running commentary on what is being acted and sung without ever being, in the *Opera and Drama* sense, subordinated to it. There is *co*-ordination of stage and orchestra, not *sub*-ordination. The motifs are germ musical ideas which are freely, nonsystematically, polyphonically developed. Their combination, variation, transformation, and interweaving are the very essence of musical improvisation: new themes are introduced where they are needed for a musical portrait of what is going on, and without careful integration into the course of the action. An example is the theme associated with the knight, Walter von Stolzing; he is on the stage from the opening curtain throughout the entire act, but the theme associated with him does not occur until well beyond the middle of the act, at the point where he is presented to the mastersingers.

When introduced, new themes are usually elaborately devel-

oped in the immediately succeeding passages with slight regard
for the details of the action on the stage. The seven pages of vocal
score which follow the first appearance of the Walter theme are
a free polyphonic development of this one motif. The short four-
note theme of uncertain designation which appears on the first
entrance of the mastersingers in Act I is likewise almost exclusively
used in the succeeding seventeen pages, after which the theme associated with Johannistag appears and is in turn freely developed.

Later on in the drama, most notably in Act III, Scene 1, all
the motifs are gathered together, and a wealth of thematic "fixed
improvisation," such as has no counterpart in any other Wagnerian
drama, is unfolded. The famous monolog of Hans Sachs in this
act, "Wahn, Wahn, überall Wahn" ("Delusion, delusion everywhere"), is a magnificent example of such free improvisation on
orchestral themes.

If more proof is needed of the loose connection between the
themes and the action of the play, to say nothing of the dialog,
which in *Opera and Drama* was intended to be the source of the
motifs, we have it in the fact that the overture to *The Mastersingers*, constructed entirely out of themes which appear throughout the work, was written first. It was performed in November
1862, before Wagner had even begun setting the poem to music.

The verse form is in comic imitation of the sixteenth-century
Knittelvers of the mastersinger period and is a far cry from the
highly alliterative concentrated verse of an exalted nature, with
irregular accent, which Wagner had hitherto used. There is no
suggestion of an attempt at alliterative or rhyming parallels or
contrasts, of condensation of speech into root syllables. The imitation of the banalities and naiveté of the rhyme and rhythm of
Knittelvers adds a constant delightful ironic overtone to the dialog:

> Lenzes Gebot, die süsse Not,
> die legt' es ihm in die Brust:
> nun sang er, wie er musst',
> und wie er musst', so konnt' er's,—
> das merkt' ich ganz besonders.
> Dem Vogel, der heut' sang,
> dem war der Schnabel hold gewachsen;

macht' er den Meistern bang',
gar wohl gefiel er doch Hans Sachsen!

(Meistersinger, 216)

(Spring's command, sweet need,
this filled his breast:
and he sang as he had to,
and as he had to, so he was able,—
that I noted in particular.
The bird who sang today,
his beak was nobly formed;
though he caused concern to the masters,
he greatly pleased Hans Sachs!)

For broadly comic effect, Wagner exaggerates the doggerel even more, especially in Beckmesser's lines, as for example:

Ich dank' euch inniglich,
weil ihr so minniglich;
für euch nur stimme ich,
kauf' eure Werke gleich,
mache zum Merker euch,
doch fein mit Kreide weich,
nicht mit dem Hammerstreich!

(Meistersinger, 428)

(I thank you sincerely,
because you are so kind;
for you alone I will vote,
I will buy your works right away,
make you a "marker,"
but with nice soft chalk,
not with hammer blows!)

This verse form does not pretend to fulfill in any single respect the qualifications which were drawn up in *Opera and Drama* for the purpose of word-tone synthesis. Nor does the musical line to which it is set contain any consistent application of the devices employed in the musical lines of the previous works. Much of the musical dialog is designed to yield the most natural declamatory rhythm and accentuation possible. Emphasis is placed on rapidity; no other work of Wagner's has such a preponderance of sixteenth notes in the vocal line. The result, if one regards the vocal line

purely as music, but apart from its rich orchestral accompaniment
and its mimetic function, is a kind of heightened recitative with
relatively little musical interest. The following is from a monolog
of Sachs near the close of the first scene of Act III:

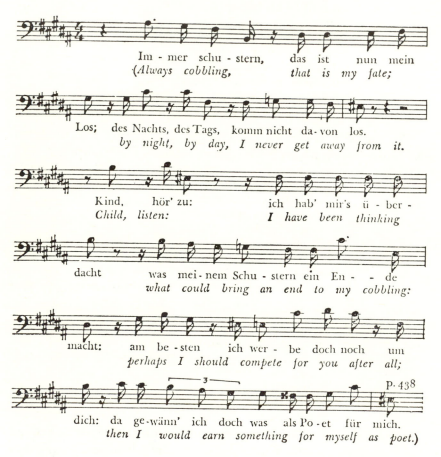

Im - mer schu - stern,   das ist   nun   mein
(Always cobbling,   *that is   my fate;*

Los;   des Nachts, des Tags, komm nicht da- von los.
by night, by day, I never get away from it.

Kind,   hör' zu: ich hab' mir's ü - ber -
Child, listen: *I have been thinking*

dacht   was mei - nem Schu - stern ein En - - de
what could bring an end to my cobbling:

macht: am be - sten   ich wer - be doch noch   um
perhaps I should compete for you after all;

p. 438

dich: da ge -wänn' ich doch was als Po - et für mich.
then I   would earn something for myself as poet.)

It is manifestly impossible to analyze this type of line on the same
basis as those in *The Rhinegold, The Valkyrie, Siegfried,* and
Tristan and Isolde. All the word-tone details found in those works
are here conspicuous by their absence. The melodic line is fashioned principally to aid in the natural delivery of the lines, an
operatic technique which Wagner had roundly condemned in
Opera and Drama, where he wrote, "Nothing of the melody remained but a musical prose, strengthening only the rhetorical ac-

cent of a verse which itself proved to be but prose." (W.S., IV, 114) This aptly illustrates the extent to which his views had changed since *Opera and Drama,* for in a late essay on *The Mastersingers,* he wrote, "If a witty friend once said that my orchestra music struck him as a continuous fugue turned into an opera, my singers and chorus members know that when they had solved their difficult musical task they had acquired the mastery of a continuous dialog which was as easy and natural for them as the most ordinary conversation; they . . . found themselves guided to the most rapid and lively interchange with the utmost naturalness." (W.S., IX, 211)

Such recitative, however, ends at the foot-lights. The orchestra is not "accompanying" these lines in the restricted sense of that word but is progressing through a series of free variations on a theme introduced earlier in the same scene, of uncertain designation but associated with Eva. Thus, the musical counterpart of the scene to which these lines belong is in the orchestra, while the music of the melodic line is part, not of the musical, but of the mimetic "improvisation." It is the opposite extreme from the kind of word-tone and vocal-orchestral balance that found its most consummate expression in Act I of *The Valkyrie,* where the melodic verse was the nucleus of an organic word-tone synthesis and the orchestra functioned as a subordinate element. On the other hand, these passages do not constitute a reversion to the precursor of melodic verse found in *Lohengrin,* as Ernest Newman suggests. (W.M.A., 279) There Wagner in his conscious effort to catch the natural speech rhythm curtailed the interest of the musical line by enforcing the strictest subordination to the words. But in *Lohengrin,* as in the early dramas, the word-tone synthesis of the melodic verse, not the orchestra, was the focal point, and thus the chief element of musical interest. In the melodic dialog of *The Mastersingers,* the word-tone combination, no longer a synthesis, is a part of the scenic action, and the orchestra supplies the musical commentary.

This kind of poetic-musical dialog forms the basic structure of the speeches of every character in every scene, except at those points where formal musical numbers occur. Here is an excerpt from the first scene, sung by Eva:

During the more reflective moments, where the dialog is paced at a more deliberate tempo, there is greater opportunity for the musical portion of the word-tone combination to assert itself. But, even here, synthesis in the *Opera and Drama* sense is not attempted, and mimetic declamation is the uppermost consideration. The following is from the famous monolog of Hans Sachs, "Wahn, Wahn, überall Wahn" ("Delusion, delusion everywhere"), in the first scene of Act III:

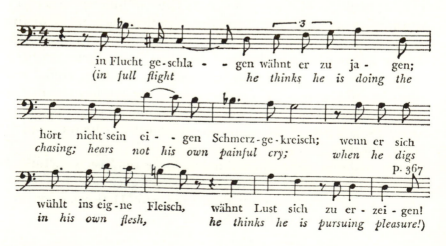

Except for the slower pace, this excerpt is quite like the two already quoted. There is no musical symmetry, no pictorialization, except possibly on the word "Schmerzgekreisch." However, in the orchestra, as these words are being sung, is to be found musical lyricism of great beauty, a contrapuntal treatment of the eloquent theme associated with Hans Sachs's mood of resignation and renunciation.

Not all the musical-poetic dialog is this severe. Wagner frequently embellishes the vocal line with pleasant musical designs. This is done rather arbitrarily, as a kind of decorative flourish which often is not related to the words it accompanies:

Doch ein - mal im Jah - - re find' ich's wei - se,
(But once a year I deem it wise

dass man die Re - geln selbst pro - bir',   ob in der Ge -
that one test the rules themselves,   to see whether

wohn - heit trä - gem Glei - se   ihr Kraft und Le -
in the lazy course of habit   their strength and life

p. 111

ben sich nicht ver - lier'!
have not diminished!)

There is symmetry and there is musical interest here, adding a degree of gracefulness and charm to the melody, but it is not related to the sense of the words. The vocal line is decorated with a little flourish at the end of each phrase, which relieves the severity characteristic of the previous examples but which is otherwise unmotivated. It is non-functional musical decoration, not word-tone synthesis. In fact, it is the unmotivated aspect of these rather simple decorative flourishes which gives them such charm. They add a musical touch of gentle irony to that of the verse, which I noted above.

The various orchestral motifs, transferred momentarily to the melodic line, are a frequent source of such musical ornamentation. Their appearance creates a refreshing contrast to the lack of musical symmetry in much of the dialog:

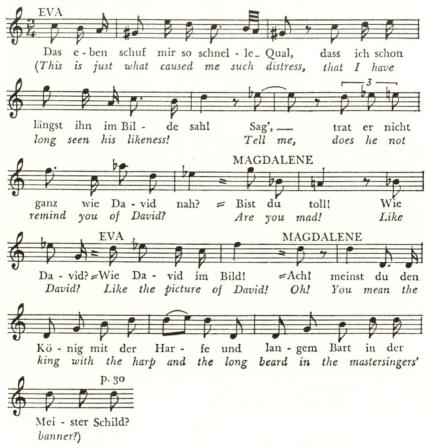

EVA

Das e - ben schuf mir so schnel - le_ Qual, dass ich schon
(*This is just what caused me such distress, that I have*

längst ihn im Bil - de sah! Sag', ___ trat er nicht
long seen his likeness! Tell me, does he not

MAGDALENE

ganz wie Da - vid nah? = Bist du toll! Wie
remind you of David? Are you mad! Like

EVA   MAGDALENE

Da - vid? =Wie Da - vid im Bild! =Ach! meinst du den
David? Like the picture of David! Oh! You mean the

Kö - nig mit der Har - fe und lan - gem Bart in der
king with the harp and the long beard in the mastersingers'

p. 30

Mei - ster Schild?
banner?)

The first eleven measures of the above are the usual rapid, musically unimportant dialog. From the word "David" in the sixth measure, the orchestra plays with the merry David theme until in the eleventh measure it changes to the motif of the mastersingers. From the twelfth measure on, the same theme also appears in the melodic line. To be noted is the contrast in poetic-musical relationship between the last few measures and the preceding part of the excerpt.

The most extended usage of this kind is the address of Veit Pogner in Act I. It is made up almost exclusively of leitmotifs. The following measures are from the end of that address:

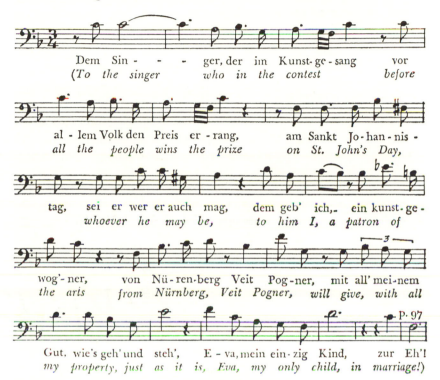

Dem Sin - - - ger, der im Kunst- ge - sang vor
(To the singer who in the contest before

al - lem Volk den Preis er - rang, am Sankt Jo - han - nis -
all the people wins the prize on St. John's Day,

tag, sei er wer er auch mag, dem geb' ich,_ ein kunst- ge -
whoever he may be, to him I, a patron of

wog'- ner, von Nü - ren-berg Veit Pog -ner, mit all' mei-nem
the arts from Nürnberg, Veit Pogner, will give, with all

Gut, wie's geh' und steh', E - va, mein ein- zig Kind, zur Eh'!
my property, just as it is, Eva, my only child, in marriage!)

p. 97

The musical pattern is very pronounced, consisting of four pairs of phrases plus a final flourish on the last words. The first phrase contains an extension, previously established by the orchestra, of the four-note motif associated with the mastersingers; the exact original motif appears on the word "Kunstgesang." The musical phrase on the words, "am Sankt Johannistag" is rhythmically a part of the Johannistag motif, which is the most prominent feature of the orchestra during this address. The words, "dem geb' ich," and the following "ein Kunstgewog'ner" are a slight adaptation of the Johannistag motif.

This is a far different technique from the musical-poetic synthesis in the earlier works. The musical line does not grow out of the poetic line, the decoration is extraneous, in the nature of an extension of the thematic variations which are being played by the orchestra.

Each of these two techniques of musical-poetic dialog can be found in those mimetic passages for chorus where the musical effect is subordinate to the stage action. The voice parts during the street-riot scene contain no recognizable musical pattern. They occur simultaneously, or they overlap, with a seeming spontaneity which is the epitome of fixed mimetic (not musical) improvisation. On the other hand, during the final scene of Act III, when the chorus registers its disapproval of Beckmesser as a contestant for the prize, their very lively dialog-like "scheint mir nicht der Rechte" has a motival musical pattern, consisting of a theme which is very prominently used in the overture:

The musical figure gives the lines a graceful swing, similar to those in Pogner's address, although not scrupulously following the poetic rhythm.

Formal musical numbers have a prominent place in *The Mastersingers*. Besides the famous prize song in its various appearances (*Meistersinger*, 289, 440, 538), other examples are Walter's trial song, "Am stillen Herd" ("At the still hearth") from Act I

(*Meistersinger*, 126); Sachs's humorous cobbling song in Act II, "Jerum! Jerum!" (*Meistersinger*, 262, 267, 272); David's song from Act III, "Am Jordan Sankt Johannes stand" ("At the Jordan St. John stood") (*Meistersinger*, 360); Beckmesser's serenade (*Meistersinger*, 297); and the magnificent quintet at the end of Act III, Scene 1 (*Meistersinger*, 458); as well as frequent shorter passages. There are also a series of formal numbers for full chorus, such as the chorale at the beginning (*Meistersinger*, 14); the homage to Hans Sachs in the closing scene (*Meistersinger*, 495), a setting of the first stanza of the historical Sachs's poem, "Die Wittembergisch Nachtigall"; the choruses of the various guilds in the final scene (*Meistersinger*, 468–82); and the imposing final chorus (*Meistersinger*, 564); as well as the songs and dances of the apprentices and journeymen scattered throughout the work.

If we were measuring the work by *Opera and Drama* we would have to condemn all these, for Wagner was very explicit in that work about such formal musical numbers. They are to disappear from the art-work of the future, he said then, for the stronger power of the musical line, when it does not closely follow the contour of the words, causes the latter to be submerged, so that the very essence of what the music is presumed to be expressing is not transmitted to the listener. It does however fit the quite different statement he makes in *Beethoven*, where he says the organic relation between words and music is an illusion. For when words are sung to music, it is not the poetic thought which is transmitted but that which the poetry "engendered in the musician as music and to music." (W.S., IX, 103. Quoted, pp. 157–58.)

Apropos of the priority of music over text, Ernest Newman, in his biography of Wagner, discusses at some length the fact that the melody of Walter's dream song was composed in its entirety before the words were written. Newman writes, "Three or four of the pages . . . of the manuscript present a curious spectacle: the melody of the Dream Song . . . is there, but without any words, although the full text of each of Sachs's interjections accompanies the music. On the 25th October . . . Wagner wrote [to King Ludwig] 'I am well into the third act now, and one of these days I shall have to write the words of Walter's Prize Song, [he means what Newman above calls the "Dream Song," which in its later

version is the Prize Song] the melody of which is already finished.' " (E.N., III, 189) Newman uses this as proof that Wagner
the artist did not take his own theoretical doctrines seriously. It
is, to be sure, a breach of the *Opera and Drama* rules; but no more
so than all the rest of *The Mastersingers*. Wagner's current thinking on the relation of text to music was far different from what
he had so passionately believed in the old days. "Music loses none
of its character even when very different texts are set to it," he
writes in *Beethoven*. (W.S., IX, 103) This is directly from Schopenhauer's *World as Will and Idea* (A.S., I, 311) and is compatible
with the rest of his later theories.

The dream song is a special case, anyway. The words had to be
written so as to yield Beckmesser's ridiculous parody of them in
the final scene, and the process of their composition of course becomes more mechanical than inspirational. This is clear from the
quality of the poetry in the dream song. We are forced to stretch
a point in order to agree with Hans Sachs in his admiration for
them, although Walter has been capable earlier in Act I of some
quite beautiful verses.

Perhaps the most convincing test of the validity of *The Destiny
of Opera* as a theoretical counterpart of *The Mastersingers* is to
attend a performance with the theory clearly in mind. It is truly
surprising how the definition "mimetic-musical improvisation of
consummate poetic value fixed by the finest artistic judgment"
seems to leap at one over and over again during the performance.
There is simply a natural affinity between the two, which is the
best proof that they are counterparts of one another.

chapter eighteen

Siegfried, Act III and Twilight of the Gods

WITH THE MASTERSINGERS finished and performed, and with the likelihood that the production of his gigantic Nibelungen cycle awaited only its completion, Wagner turned back to where he had left off in 1857, at the beginning of Act III of *Siegfried*. The work progressed steadily along with the plans for its performance, and in 1872 it was finished except for the scoring of the *Twilight of the Gods*. The first performances were given at Wagner's Festival Theater in Bayreuth in the summer of 1876.

Twelve years lie between Acts II and III of *Siegfried,* and in general it is amazing how successfully Wagner worked himself back into the style of the *Ring.* But closer inspection shows the unmistakable influence of those intervening years, and the effect of the quite differing techniques of *Tristan and Isolde* and *The Mastersingers.* In fact, *Siegfried,* Act III, and *Twilight of the Gods* are a fascinating, not to say bewildering, mixture of three Wagnerian styles; and anyone who attempts to analyze these works from a single point of view is in for trouble.

Since he was returning to a poem which was directly influenced by *Opera and Drama,* and to a musical score of which hundreds of pages had been written in accordance with that theory, it is not surprising that Wagner's style in this last portion of the *Ring* shows evidence of the three-fold synthesis of his earlier theory, which in *The Mastersingers* he had virtually abandoned. On the other hand, coming to the *Ring* after the composition of *The Mastersingers* and his personal supervision of its première in Munich, interrupting his work on it to write the essays *Beethoven* and *The Destiny of Opera,* Wagner could hardly have avoided the influence of his mimetic theory in his new work. Finally, it can be shown that certain passages, particularly the love duets from Act III of *Siegfried* and the prologue of *Twilight of the Gods,* are in the *Tristan* vein.

A difference is at once noticeable in the prelude to Act III of *Siegfried.* Here only the old *Ring* motifs are used, but their combination and musical treatment are bolder, freer and more lavish than in any of the preludes to the previous acts of the *Ring* dramas. No less than nine familiar motifs are brought into this short introduction, a considerably higher concentration than in any of the others, and they are combined with an improvisational freedom which reminds one of *The Mastersingers* orchestra far more than the earlier *Ring.* This heralds a noticeable difference in the use of leitmotifs throughout; they are used in a profusion which is not in evidence even in the first two acts of *Siegfried,* where we already noted a deviation from the strict use that characterized *The Rhinegold* and *The Valkyrie.* The motifs come at one in such swift succession, often combined, that it is impossible to associate them, as they were originally intended, with reminiscences of previous scenes. In Act III of *Siegfried,* for instance, as the hero is ascending the mountain to Brünnhilde's rock, the Slumber motif from *The Valkyrie,* Siegfried's Horn Call from *Siegfried,* the Bird Call from *Siegfried,* and the Bondage motif from *The Rhinegold* are contrapuntally interwoven into a single measure. Three-fold and four-fold combinations of this kind are numerous. Because of this more lavish use of leitmotif, the total number of separate occurrences is much higher than in the earlier *Ring* dramas. The number in *Twilight of the Gods* (1003) is more than double the number in *The Valkyrie* (405). (Immediate repetitions in the same scene or portion of a scene are not included in these figures.)

Certain orchestra passages, clearly parallel to *The Mastersingers* style of composition, are not so much concerned with intricate interweaving of themes as with free symphonic variation of one or two motifs, often extending over several pages of the score. The interlude known as "Siegfried's Rhine Journey" is an excellent example of this, with its waltz-like treatment of Siegfried's Horn Call. The same motif is freely and exuberantly varied in the beginning of Scene 2, Act III. Similar examples are the Heroic Love motif used at the close of Act II, Scene 4; of the Bird motif at the beginning of Act III, Scene 2 of *Siegfried;* or of the Magic Fire motif heard frequently throughout *Twilight of the Gods.* The famous funeral music between Scene 2 and 3 of *Twilight of the Gods* is by contrast more clearly an example of the kind of contrapuntal interweaving in the style of *Siegfried* and the earlier *Ring.*

Wagner has become quite careless in his use of leitmotif. There are literally hundreds of cases where one is used either with a loose thread of connection or in disregard of the connotation which its use as a motif of reminiscence had established. The Charmed Sleep motif from *The Valkyrie,* Act III, is brilliantly announced by full orchestra immediately after Brünnhilde has ridden Grane into Siegfried's blazing funeral pyre at the close of the final scene. In Scene 1 of Act III of *Siegfried,* when Wotan says to Erda, "Bekannt ist dir was die Tiefe birgt, was Berg und Tal, Luft und Wasser durchwebt" ("Known to you is what the depths conceal, what inhabits mountain and valley, air and water"), the orchestra plays the accompanying figure from Siegmund's Spring Song of *The Valkyrie.* In the same scene, when Wotan says, "Im Zwange der Welt weben die Nornen" ("In bondage to the world weave the Norns"), the orchestra plays the Ring motif. A few leitmotifs are unintentionally comic. Thus, the exquisite Love theme of Siegmund and Sieglinde from Act I of *The Valkyrie* is heard in the prologue of *Twilight of the Gods* when Brünnhilde expresses her affection for her horse, Grane. (*Götterdämmerung,* 32) Then there is the notorious example of the Dragon motif, which inexplicably enters during the passionate closing section of the love duet from *Siegfried,* Act III, as Brünnhilde sings, "Wie mein Blick dich verzehrt . . . wie mein Arm dich presst" ("As my glance devours you, as my arm presses you"). (*Siegfried,* 329) In spite of these and many similar examples, the fiction of functional use of leitmotif in the later works persists. Ernest Newman in *Wagner as Man and Artist* says, "The astounding tissue of the

Götterdämmerung teems with transitions of the most abrupt kind; but they are all intelligible because the physiognomies of the leit-motives are familiar to us, and every allusion is instantaneously clear. Their logic is only partly in themselves, and partly in the poetic ideas of which they are symbols." (W.M.A., 241)

There are, to be sure, a number of powerful functional usages in the *Opera and Drama* sense, although these are decidedly in the minority. Thus, the awesome descending scale of the motif known as the "End of the Gods," which originally appeared in *The Rhinegold* with Erda's prophetic words, "Alles, was ist, endet! Ein düst'rer Tag dämmert den Göttern!" ("All that is will end! A gloomy day dawns for the gods!") (*Rheingold,* 194), is heard in the dramatic pause after Siegfried's sword has split Wotan's spear, the symbol of his rule. (*Siegfried,* 279) The sinister motif of Al-berich's curse from *The Rhinegold* is sounded as Hagen thrusts his spear into Siegfried's back. (*Götterdämmerung,* 296) Hagen's initial greeting to Siegfried in Act I, "Heil Siegfried, teurer Held" ("Hail Siegfried, noble hero") is ominously set to the contours of this Curse motif. (*Götterdämmerung,* 61)

The new motifs, those which first appear in *Siegfried,* Act III on, are of a quite different nature from the earlier *Ring* motifs. They are broader, longer, more independently musical, with less emphasis on characteristic pictorialization than the briefer, more fragmentary, earlier ones. They are unsuitable for the kind of psychological commentary Wagner had used the earlier motifs for. The motif known as the "Volsungs' Heritage," for example,

Siegfried, p. 257

is unlike any previously introduced. Of a similar nature are those known as "Ecstasy"; "Song of Peace"; "Siegfried, Protector of the World"; "Song of Death"; "Heroic Love," etc.

There is only one example of a motif of reminiscence in the *Opera and Drama* sense, the Penalty motif:

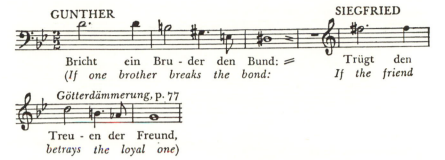

GUNTHER   SIEGFRIED

Bricht   ein   Bru - der   den   Bund: Trügt   den
(If   one   brother   breaks   the   bond: If   the   friend

Götterdämmerung, p. 77

Treu - en   der   Freund,
betrays   the   loyal   one)

It occurs only nine times after its first appearance in the melodic line, each time with the purpose of linking emotionally the new scene in which it appears to the scene of the oath and to the original words. Its somber intervals are heard, for instance, after Hagen has plunged his spear into Siegfried's back. During Gunther's bewildered question, "Hagen, was tatest du?" ("Hagen, what have you done?") and Hagen's defiant "Meineid rächt' ich!" ("Treachery I have avenged!"), the orchestra intones the motif in a gradual crescendo. (*Götterdämmerung*, 297) There are several other new leitmotifs derived from the melodic verse, but in every other case they are used indiscriminately in succeeding scenes, and the force of the derivation thus breaks down.

The poem, of course, having been written in 1852, is like those of the earlier *Ring* dramas, with a highly alliterative, concentrated form of verse in the tradition of *Opera and Drama*. There are more functional alliterative groupings than in *The Rhinegold*, or in Acts I and II of *Siegfried*, although fewer than in the poem of *The Valkyrie*, which in this respect is the richest of all the *Ring* poems. But, significantly, only a few of these are carried out also in musical terms by a functional adaptation of the musical line. We have seen this kind of word-tone synthesis to be a prominent characteristic of the earlier *Ring* dramas, and it is a sure sign of a change in technique that even ready-made examples are ignored by Wagner this time.

There are instances, and very effective ones indeed, of the old musical-poetic synthesis, but they are strikingly less numerous than in the earlier *Ring*. The following, sung by Brünnhilde, from *Twilight of the Gods*, Act II, is one:

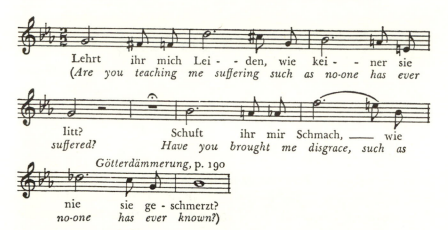

Lehrt ihr mich Lei - - den, wie kei - - ner sie
(*Are you teaching me suffering such as no-one has ever*

litt?   Schuft   ihr mir Schmach, _____ wie
suffered?   *Have you brought me disgrace, such as*

Götterdämmerung, p. 190

nie   sie ge - schmerzt?
no-one   has ever known?)

The force of the alliterative parallelism ("lehrt—Leiden—litt," "schuft—Schmach—geschmerzt"), as well as the parallel construction of the two verses as a whole, is intensified by the sequences of the musical line. The two key words, "Leiden" and "Schmach," are made the center of attention by the contour of the melody. The distorted intervals and the rather tortured chromatics of the melody communicate musically the strained effect which the words express. The melodic line is a variant of the motif of reminiscence derived from the melodic verse of *The Valkyrie,* Act III, "War es so schmählich, was ich verbrach?" etc. (*Walküre,* 265) The force of the distortion is thus strengthened by contrast with the smoother contours of the original motif.

The following, sung by Brünnhilde in the early part of Act I, is an excellent example of the *Opera and Drama* technique of synthesis:

Ging sein Lauf mit mir _____ einst kühn durch die Lüf -
(*If his course with me   once went boldly through*

- te,   mit mir   ver- lor _____ es die mäch - t'ge
the air,   with me   he lost   this great power;

There is a vivid contrast between the two halves of each line, parallel to the contrasts in the verse. In each case, the vigorous rhythm of the Valkyries' horses underlies the first half of the line. The orchestral accompaniment strengthens the rhythm by a dotted figure and sweeping string passages, which are kept *piano* so as not to overbalance. In the second half of each line, the melody has no energy. It is much less rhythmic, more sustained, and thus intensifies the force of the poetic contrast. The orchestral accompaniment also changes abruptly in each case to measure-long sustained chords.

The following is taken from Hagen's magnificent monolog at the close of Scene 2, Act I of *Twilight of the Gods:*

The musical line of "Ihr freien Söhne, frohe Gesellen" communicates the grim irony behind the words by a certain suavity which contains an ominous undertone. The deliberate step-wise ascending progression on "segelt nur lustig dahin" evokes the exact opposite of "lustig," and becomes a poetic-musical expression of Hagen's sardonic humor. The whole ends on a threateningly sinister note with the pitch accentuation of "dient" and the prolongation of "Nibelungen." Below the final lines, from "dient" to the end, the orchestra plays the severely distorted Valhalla theme first heard in *The Valkyrie*, when Wotan revealed to Brünnhilde Erda's oracular words, "Wenn der Liebe finst'rer Feind zürnend zeugt einen Sohn, der Sel'gen Ende säumt dann nicht" ("When love's black enemy angrily engenders a son, the blessed ones' end delays not then"). (*Walküre*, 128) The two moments, past and present, are thus functionally linked by the appearance of the leitmotif in the orchestra.

The following impressive excerpt from *Siegfried* is sung by the hero just before he awakens Brünnhilde with a kiss:

Siegfried, p. 294

The serenely beautiful opening phrase is followed at (2) by a melodic line which expresses a certain degree of awakening agitation because of its less smoothly progressing intervals and more irregular rhythm, to correspond with the words "mild erzitternd" and "Zagen." At (3) the musical line becomes decidedly more impassioned, mainly by virtue of the stronger syncopation, as Siegfried approaches the sleeping Brünnhilde. This forms a transition to the impulsive outbreak at (4), which constitutes the preliminary climax. After a meaningful pause, the simple musical-poetic synthesis at (5) offers a strikingly effective contrast. There follows the chief climax at (6). The downward course of the melodic line at (7) communicates the force of the submission implied by the words. This is genuine word-tone synthesis in the true *Opera and Drama* spirit, such as cannot be found anywhere in *The Mastersingers.*

Much of the dialog is not like this, however, showing rather the influence of *The Mastersingers* mimetic technique, which aims at rapid, life-like dialog, as in the following:

(*Götterdämmerung*, p. 67)

This poetic-melodic style is a kind of compromise between the melodic verse of the former *Ring* and the dialog-like vocal line of *The Mastersingers*. It is not as rapid as the undecorated dialog of the latter work. It has a certain breadth which brings it into closer proximity to the early *Ring* style. But such passages do not incorporate the specific features which gave meaning to the word-tone design of the early *Ring,* since these would be incompatible with the comparatively swift-moving mimetic representation. The rather amorphous quality which results from the cross-purposes of the two styles characterizes many pages of the score of *Twilight of the Gods:* Act I, Scene 1, pp. 45–60; large portions of Scene 2, pp. 61–68; Act II, Scene 2, pp. 142–50; Act II, Scene 5, pp. 211–18; and pp. 305–14 of the final scene.

The absence of the "answering unit" in many pages of *Twilight of the Gods,* complementary phrases that give a satisfying symmetry to the vocal line, is undoubtedly the result of the mixing of styles. An excellent comparison in this regard is between Alberich's dialog in *Siegfried,* Act II, and in *Twilight of the Gods,* Act II. In the latter, the mimetic influence dominates so that there is little symmetry. In the former, though the dialog is vivid, appropriately ugly, and harsh during the bickering of the two dwarfs, the answering patterns underlie the dialog sufficiently to give the vocal line symmetry. Even the dialog of the heroic characters can be used to illustrate this lack of symmetry in *Twilight of the Gods.*

The following is sung by Siegfried to Gutrune on his return from Brünnhilde's rock:

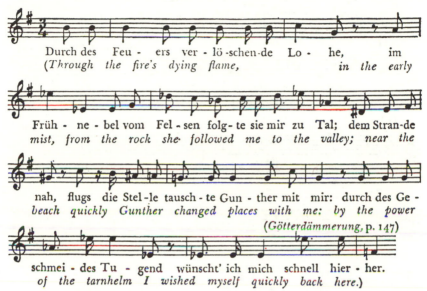

Durch des Feu - ers ver - lö -schen-de Lo - he, im
(Through the fire's dying flame, in the early

Früh - ne - bel vom Fel - sen folg- te sie mir zu Tal; dem Stran-de
mist, from the rock she followed me to the valley; near the

nah, flugs die Stel -le tausch - te Gun - ther mit mir: durch des Ge -
beach quickly Gunther changed places with me: by the power

(*Götterdämmerung*, p. 147)

schmei - des Tu - gend wünscht' ich mich schnell hier - her.
of the tarnhelm I wished myself quickly back here.)

A very prominent feature of the vocal line in *Siegfried*, Act III and *Twilight of the Gods* is nonfunctional musical decoration by graceful musical flourishes, or use of the leitmotif figures for the same purpose, which we remember Wagner to have used prominently in *The Mastersingers*. Reproduced below are six examples to serve for the hundreds which exist in the two works:

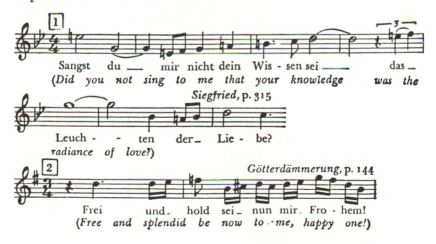

Sangst du — mir nicht dein Wis - sen sei —— das —
(Did you not sing to me that your knowledge was the

Siegfried, p. 315

Leuch - - ten der— Lie - be?
radiance of love?)

Götterdämmerung, p. 144

Frei und— hold sei— nun mir— Fro - hem!
(Free and splendid be now to me, happy one!)

jagt   er   auf   Ta -   ten   won- nig   um -   her,
(he   joyously   seeks   adventure)

sei -ne   Knie'   um -win- dend   lie - gen wir   Wal - kü - 'ren,
(embracing   his   knees   lie   we   Valkyries)

dankt __   dir __   ge - wiss   nöch   das   Weib.
(the   woman   will   surely   thank   you.)

Durch   dei - ne _   Tu - - gend al - lein _   soll so __   ich
(Through   your   virtue   alone   shall   I   do

Ta -   ten noch   wir - ken?
my   deeds?)

(*1*) is from *Siegfried*. The verse is sung to the motif of the Volsungs'
Heritage (quoted, p. 192). There is no functional reason for the
appearance of the motif, and it is quite obvious in the distortion
of the poetic declamation that a musical pattern and not a poetic-
musical unit is being worked out. (2) is not a motif, but merely
one of the many embellishments that occur throughout *Twilight
of the Gods*. (3) is sung by Hagen. It is the motif of Siegfried's
Horn Call. (4) is sung by Waltraute in her great scene from Act I.
It is the motif of Wotan's Rage in *The Valkyrie*. The vivid picture
of Wotan that Waltraute paints before Brünnhilde in this scene
is at the very opposite extreme from the anger that the motif was
originally intended to express. (5) is part of the motif of Heroic
Love from the prologue of *Twilight of the Gods*. It appears in full

in the orchestra at the same time. At this point it is used with no concrete association as a purely musical embellishment.

A prominent influence of *The Mastersingers* style are the concerted numbers in *Twilight of the Gods:* the chorus of the vassals in Act II, which has a very *Mastersingers*-like swing; the trio of conspirators at the end of Act II; and the very melodious song of the Rhine maidens, particularly at its close, where Siegfried joins in a tuneful obligato.

The *Tristan* influence is easy to see in the two love duets between Brünnhilde and Siegfried. The following is from *Siegfried,* Act III. A like technique is used in the prologue to *Twilight of the Gods:*

It can be seen from this analysis that Wagner was unable to turn back the clock completely, that his efforts to recapture the earlier style inevitably ran into the roadblock of the later influences. How foolish to attempt to relate the style of *Siegfried*, Act III and *Twilight of the Gods* exclusively to *Opera and Drama* and the earlier *Ring* dramas!

chapter nineteen

Parsifal

THERE SEEMS to be no middle ground about Wagner's last great work. It is either fiercely admired or fiercely attacked. Even performances tend to extremes. A good performance is magical, a bad one (most are bad) unbearable. For in *Parsifal* the tempo is slow and deliberate, the measure stately and solemn, the drama subdued and stylized. Wagner rightly characterized it as a *Bühnenweihfestspiel* (Consecrational Festival Play). In many ways, it is more of a pageant than a drama; it has the epic breadth and pace of a pageant. A quasi-religious atmosphere predominates. The air of sanctimoniousness which accompanies some *Parsifal* performances is hard for many opera goers to live with. It is symbolized by the tradition, begun at Bayreuth, of not applauding after the Grail scenes which end the first and last acts. The audience is expected to withdraw in hushed silence. This custom invariably runs into trouble, even at Bayreuth (though there to a lesser extent). There are always at least a few uninitiated who break the silence with some tentative hand-clapping. This brings down upon them wrathful hissing from the faithful until quiet is restored.

Wagner hoped that the work would be reserved for his own Festival Theater at Bayreuth, and the defiance of his wish by the Metropolitan Opera House, where the first performance outside Bayreuth was given on Christmas Eve in 1903, was a matter of world-wide controversy. Of course, the work could not permanently remain the private preserve of Bayreuth, but once one has experienced the inevitable difference in atmosphere between a festival performance there and a regular repertory performance elsewhere, one can see that Wagner's intuition was sound.

Parsifal is the only work of Wagner's to be written after the

erection of the Festival Theater at Bayreuth and the performance
of the first festival in 1876, and it shows their unmistakable influence. In the Festival Theater Wagner had constructed the il-
lusionist opera stage par excellence, with a sunken invisible orchestra, whose sounds emerge already blended into an auditorium
unparalleled in acoustical properties. The stage, with nothing intervening between it and the spectator, who is in total darkness, takes
on the vividness of a dream-picture.

Parsifal, born directly out of these conditions, is a splendid
illustration of the *Beethoven* theory, which argued a synthesis of
music and visual action as complementary revelations or objectifications of the metaphysical will. The poet-composer's clairvoyant
vision of the essence of the universe is the single impulse which
is simultaneously transmitted in two complementary ways, in terms
of visual drama and in terms of music. "The world of one," Wagner wrote in that essay, "completely coincides with the world of
the other, so that each is contained in the other, even though they
seem to move in entirely separate spheres." (W.S., IX, 107) Each is
therefore in its own way an expression of the clairvoyant vision of
the metaphysical will. The spectator who keeps this relationship
in mind during a performance, particularly under the conditions
at Bayreuth, will find his appreciation of the work greatly en-
hanced.

The orchestra in *Parsifal* is a kind of Greek chorus. It does less
"accompanying" than in any other work of Wagner. It functions
more as a simultaneous commentator on the action. From it seems
to emerge the acoustical counterpart of the visual action. "The
music sounds, and what it sounds, you see on the stage" (W.S.,
IX, 305), Wagner wrote in an essay, "On the Term 'Music-
Drama,'" in 1872, and *Parsifal* is a wonderful illustration of this.
The orchestra music is exceedingly rich and symphonic in character. In the third act, especially, there is a harmonic complexity
and daring which exceeds anything else Wagner ever wrote, even
Tristan, Act III. It supports his contention that only by being
joined with a dramatic action can music realize itself to the fullest.
Composers of symphonic music, he argued, have failed to plumb
the depths of harmonic possibilities because there was no compelling reason for them to do so.

With a few notable exceptions, the dialog in *Parsifal* is not as important as in Wagner's other works. A good indication of this is the length of the poem. Although *Parsifal* is one of the longest of the dramas in performance time, the poem is by far the shortest. Much of the action proceeds without dialog, particularly in the solemn pageantry of the Grail scenes. Here the invisible voices of the off-stage choruses, stationed at various levels above and behind the stage, float out over the scene and mingle with the rich orchestra, producing a remarkably architectural acoustical effect which is a perfect aural counterpart to the lofty church-like atmosphere of the Fortress of the Grail with its high columns.

When dialog does occur, it is often of secondary importance, as during the entire first scene of the third act, where almost all that is significant is done in pantomime. Kundry, a central figure throughout this extended scene, utters only a single word, "dienen!" The mimetic action is a series of scenic pictures: Parsifal's solemn entrance; his long silent prayer before the sacred spear; the washing of his feet in the sacred spring; the symbolic sprinkling of the holy water on Parsifal's head by Gurnemanz; the anointing of his feet and head with oil; Parsifal's baptism of Kundry; the Good Friday Spell which follows; all of which leads into the musical-scenic transformation to the final scene in the Fortress of the Grail. All of this is paralleled by an orchestral texture so rich and varied that one is compelled to think of the stage picture as "ersichtlich gewordene Taten der Musik" ("acts of music become visible"), as Wagner called his dramas in the aforementioned essay.

The verse of the *Parsifal* poem is the freest and most varied Wagner ever wrote. It runs the gamut in variety from what could be called rhythmic prose in the more epic, narrative sections:

> Ja, wann oft lange sie uns ferne blieb,
> dann brach ein Unglück wohl herein.
> Und lang schon kenn' ich sie,
> doch Titurel kennt sie noch länger.
> Der fand, als er die Burg dort baute,
> sie schlafend hier im Waldgestrüpp,
> erstarrt, leblos, wie tot.
> So fand ich selbst sie letztlich wieder,
> als uns das Unheil kaum gescheh'n,

das jener Böse über den Bergen
so schmählich über uns gebracht.   (*Parsifal*, 28)

(Yes, often when she was away from us for a long time
misfortune broke upon us.
And I know her a long time,
but Titurel knows her longer.
He found, when he built the fortress there,
her sleeping here in the underbrush,
rigid, lifeless, as though dead.
So I found her myself recently,
when the disaster had scarcely occurred
which that evil one over the mountains
so shamefully brought upon us.)

to passages of Nietzschean expressionistic intensity:

Amfortas!
Die Wunde!—die Wunde!
Sie brennt in meinem Herzen.—
Oh! Klage! Klage!
Furchtbare Klage!
Aus tiefstem Herzen schreit sie mir auf.
Oh!—Oh!
Elender!—
Jammervollster!
Die Wunde seh' ich bluten,
nun blutet sie in mir!
Hier!—hier!   (*Parsifal*, 184)

(Amfortas!
The wound!—the wound!
It burns in my heart.—
Oh! lament! lament!
Fearful lament!
From the deepest depths of my heart it cries out.
Oh!—Oh!
Miserable one!—
Most pitiable one!
The wound I see bleeding,
now it bleeds in me!
Here!—here!)

Rhyme is used; about one third of the lines are rhymed, but in a
very relaxed way, not at all in the special manner of the *Tristan*
lines. There is something about their sonorities which fits well

into the stately religious atmosphere of the work. There is an approximately equal division between verses with a regular rhythm and those with a free rhythm. Alliteration is not present, except in a few minor instances.

In the musical setting of this dialog, Wagner again runs the gamut, drawing freely on all his various techniques and blending them masterfully. There is a general regard for naturalistic declamation and a free use of the various *Opera and Drama* devices for emotional intensification but without any rigid adherence to them. The line is often, especially at climactic moments, decorated with motifs or borrowings from them, as we have seen from *The Mastersingers* on. These in the strict sense distort the natural accent, but only to the greater effectiveness and expressiveness of the vocal line and never to the degree that was noted in *The Mastersingers* (see illustration, p. 184) and some portions of *Twilight of the Gods* (see illustration, pp. 199–200).

There are a few—only a few—bare spots with quite recitative-like passages, for which little if anything can be claimed:

This is sung by Gurnemanz, to whose lot fall most of the narrative passages, in which there is a lighter musical interest. But for the most part, his narrative lines are set with more pleasing contours and a genuine if quiet musical interest. The slow pace gives the musical aspect of such lines a better chance to assert itself than in the clipped delivery of *The Mastersingers,* for example. Gurnemanz is often considered a bore by the opera listener, and he often is; he need not be so, however, any more than Wotan need be so in his great narrative in *The Valkyrie,* or King Marke in Act II of *Tristan.* This is the fault of the performer rather than the composer. It is a difficult role, but a glorious one if well performed.

Just as the *Parsifal* orchestra shows the most advanced harmony and the poem the most expressionistic poetry, so too the musical dialog at times strives for a degree of expressivity and emotional impact which exceeds any in the earlier works. In those passages, particularly Amfortas' and Kundry's lines, Wagner writes more daringly than he has ever done before, even in *Tristan,* squeezing the last ounce of emotional intensity out of the music:

den Un - - sel' - - gen, Schmach - · lü - - ster-nen,
(the   wretched   one,   eager   for   disgrace,

P. 237

den ich ver-lach - te,   lach - te, –   lach - te,–   ha - ha!
whom   I   derided,   laughed   at,   laughed,   ha   ha!)

The desperation and convulsiveness of Kundry's outburst are powerfully captured by the strained line, plunging downward crazily five times in succession, and the fragmentation on the repeated "lachte," culminating in the almost frenzied "ha-ha," high in the vocal register. This kind of vocal line vividly illustrates Guido Adler's comment that Wagner was less susceptible to beauty than to energy of expression. (Adler, 164)

By the use of off-beat entrances, long pauses, and irrational intervals, he attains some remarkably intense effects. The most striking is perhaps Kundry's revelation that she had laughed at Christ on the Cross:

Ich sah   Ihn __   Ihn __   und
(*I saw*   *Him*   *Him*   *and*

p. 225

lach - te   da traf mich   sein Blick
laughed   *then struck me*   *his glance* —)

Her sense of horror is vividly conveyed by the halting delivery of each syllable and especially by the crassness of the shrill "lachte," with its astounding interval of almost two octaves, followed by a prolonged silence.

In *Parsifal* Wagner makes very frequent use of the device we have seen him use increasingly, the transferal of an orchestral motif or a variant of it to the musical line. Whereas in *The Mastersingers* and *Twilight of the Gods* this was often done as a more or less decorative effect, and often with considerable distortion of the declamation, in *Parsifal* there are many examples where a powerful dramatic effect is attained, and the distortion of the declamation is slight. An excellent example of this is the illustration on page 212 below.

Occasionally, but always for special reasons, the orchestra phrase, transferred to the vocal line, dominates over the declamation completely. Thus, in the ritual-like words of Gurnemanz as he sprinkles water from the sacred spring on Parsifal's head, the line is sung to the Benediction motif:

p. 276

Ge - seg - - - net sei, du   Rei -ner, durch das   Rei - ne!
(*Blessed   be thou, pure one, by what is pure!*)

One of the most poignant moments and a most effective word-tone synthesis is Kundry's narrative of the death of Herzeleide:

Sie harr-te Nächt' und Ta - ge,   bis ihr ver-stummt die
(She   waited   day   and   night   until   her   lament

Kla - ge,   der   Gram — ihr zehr - te den   Schmerz;   um stil-len
grew   silent,   grief   consumed   her   pain;   for a

Tod   sie   warb: ihr   brach das Leid   das   Herz—   und
quiet death she   longed: sorrow   broke   her   heart   and

p. 207

Her - ze - lei - de   starb,
Herzeleide   died,)

These measures and those which immediately precede contain the
strongest reminiscence of word-tone synthesis in the *Opera and
Drama* sense in the entire *Parsifal* score. The musical line here
creates a poignant emotional extension of the verse expressing
Herzeleide's grief at loss of her son and her eventual sorrowful
death. The subordinate orchestra provides genuine harmonic
elucidation, especially during the first measures, in the intervals
of which a monotonously repeated major second by the wood-winds
adds to the desolate picture of Herzeleide's hopeless waiting.

A strong indication of the correctness of the interpretation of
Parsifal as a dualistic synthesis of orchestra and stage action is the
treatment of leitmotif. All the motifs in *Parsifal,* with one exception, originate in the orchestra, independent of any vocal line,
and for the most part not associated with any specific scene. They
are not motifs of reminiscence in any sense. Their predominant
character is that of a symphonic theme with no definite conceptual
connotation. As in *Tristan* and *The Mastersingers,* this permits a
high degree of freedom in their use. The theme which opens the
prelude, associated with the Eucharist because it is the melody to

which the words, "Nehmet hin meinen Leib" etc. ("Take ye my body" etc.), are later sung, is one of the central motifs of the drama. But it is by no means intended by Wagner that the idea of the Lord's Supper be conjured up by the listeners every time they hear the motif. To give it a definite label is not only pointless, but misleading, because it implies the validity of a kind of technique which is demonstrably not valid in *Parsifal*. Sections of this sustained motif yield several other important ones, principally that commonly known as "The Spear," and another of very vague connotation, usually called "Suffering." These and other motifs are varied and combined freely and symphonically with no slavish attention to the text and without functioning as leitmotifs in the strict sense at all.

If it is true, as I have tried to show, that from *Tristan* on Wagner no longer uses motifs consistently as leitmotifs in the *Opera and Drama* sense, it is a critical error first to assign them all specific names and then proceed to show how he used them wrongly. This Ernest Newman does. In *Wagner as Man and Artist*, he discusses the theme which he, as well as others, has labelled "Galloping." He catalogs every repetition of this theme to show its misuse. It is heard, for example, when Kundry hurries to the spring to draw water for the fainting Parsifal. It is heard when the Flower Maidens appear in Act II (although here, unfortunately, the association is often not far wrong) and when Kundry calls to Klingsor for help at the end of Act II. But, as has been repeatedly pointed out, this game could be played with almost any motif from *Tristan and Isolde* on, and indicates, not that Wagner has grown careless, but that his technique has altered, and that it is wrong to label such motifs and then attempt to associate the label at each repetition.

Other themes, the theme of the Holy Grail, for instance, or those associated with Kundry, Klingsor, and Parsifal, are quite clearly related to persons or things and are used only when the specific reference is inferable, though not, of course, as motifs of reminiscence, since they are not associated with a specific text or scene, and their appearance does not recall anything from the past. They are rather only musical parallels to the person or thing seen or of which mention is made. There is one motif, the so-called

"Promise" motif, which is derived in true *Opera and Drama* fashion from the vocal line and functions consistently as a reminiscence of the words to which it is first sung:

"Durch Mit - leid   wis - send,   der   rei -   ne   Tor —"
(*"By   compassion   knowing,   the   pure   fool —")*

It is used only sparingly, less than twenty times, in contrast to the hundreds of times the other motifs are heard, and on each repetition serves to bring the emotional equivalent of the words, "Durch Mitleid wissend, der reine Tor" ("By compassion knowing, the pure fool") into the consciousness of the listener. Thus, when Klingsor calls Kundry to prepare for Parsifal's arrival in his magic garden, it is heard in the orchestra and in the vocal line as well as in the words, "Den Gefährlichsten gilt's nun heut' zu besteh'n, ihn schirmt der Torheit Schild" ("The most dangerous one needs be overcome today; he is protected by the shield of foolishness"):

Den Ge -   fähr -   - lich - sten gilt's nun heut' zu be -
(*The   most   dangerous   one   needs   be   overcome   today:*

steh'n: _   ihn schirmt der Tor - heit   Schild. _
he   is   protected   by   the   shield   of   foolishness.)

It is especially effective in this scene, the music to which is for the most part a tissue of the motifs associated with Klingsor and his magic. Another powerful statement comes as Kundry uses all her seductive powers to overcome Parsifal. When the latter sings, "Auf Ewigkeit wärst du verdammt mit mir für eine Stunde Vergessens meiner Sendung in deines Arms Umfangen" ("In eternity you would be damned with me for one hour of forgetfulness of my mission in your arms' embrace") the Promise motif is heard in the orchestra and in the vocal line as well.

The music in *Parsifal* is more symphonic than in any other of Wagner's works. It is at the farthest extreme from *The Rhinegold* and *Lohengrin,* where the word came to its greatest dominance over the other elements of the synthesis. We have already seen that in 1849, after *Lohengrin,* Wagner made extensive plans for a spoken drama without musical dialog. We have seen further that from that point on he turned in the opposite direction, toward the ascendancy of tone over word. This culminates in *Parsifal.* There is a striking analogy in the fact that Wagner intended, after the completion of Parsifal, to turn to a form of pure music and write a symphony. Death came to the composer before he could carry out his plan. *Parsifal* was presented to the world in a series of sixteen performances at Bayreuth in the summer of 1882. The conductor, Hermann Levi, fell ill during the last act of the final performance and Wagner took over the baton for the closing scene. Less than five months later, on February 13, 1883, he died in Venice at the age of sixty-nine.

chapter twenty

After Parsifal

IN THIS ANALYSIS of the Wagnerian synthesis I have tried to show that one must take the whole view in order to understand fully what Wagner created in his major works; that this is an essential means for discovering important relationships which are at the very root of Wagner's artistic communication. It cannot be said that there is, or ever has been, general understanding of this fact. The Wagnerian musical drama is, for better or for worse, a creation the performance of which is entirely dependent upon opera companies, and the temptation to treat it from the musical point of view, to disregard the larger cultural context and especially the matter of art synthesis, except in the casual way this applies to all opera, is very great. This is, of course, understandable, even if unfortunate, since the audience for his works is likewise overwhelmingly musical, not to say operatic, in its tastes and expectations; but it is none the less an incomplete view, if the analysis of theory and practice in this book is accepted as valid.

The mountain of writing on Wagner has likewise been produced overwhelmingly by musicians and musicologists, who are inclined to neglect or undervalue the non-musical side of Wagner and largely ignore the idea of a synthesis of the arts. The contributions of non-musical writers are even more subject to distortion, for when one fails to give the musical side of Wagner or his works central consideration, one is indeed offering a partial view. This inclination to atomize, so to speak, Wagner's *Gesamtkunstwerk* was operative even in his own day, and it explains why the effect of his theory and practice of art synthesis has been relatively slight.

Wagner's influence has been a powerful one, but it has been largely on composers *as* composers. The list of opera writers who are indebted to him would include many major names and a myriad of forgotten ones. Even the arch-anti-Wagnerian Debussy, who wrote his sole opera, *Pelleas and Melisande,* somewhat as an act of repudiation of Wagner, did not succeed in emancipating himself, hard as he tried. "The ghost of old Klingsor, alias Richard Wagner, keeps peeping out," he complained while at work on the opera. Many composers have adapted various aspects of his musical style, his leitmotifs, his harmonies, his instrumentation, his voice leading (and most of all the love music from *Tristan and Isolde*), but without serious regard for his theories, indeed in most cases without more than the most casual knowledge of them. For the combination of theoretician, poet, conductor and composer embodied by Wagner has no parallel in the entire history of the musical stage.

For a considerable time in the late nineteenth century, when the Wagnerian musical dramas were enjoying their greatest prestige, a large number of opera composers emulated the poet-composer by writing their own texts. None of these was particularly successful, most are forgotten. The most prominent were Vincent d'Indy, with his *Fervaal* and *The Stranger,* and perhaps Siegfried, Wagner's own son, whose *Bärenhäuter* was the first and best of twelve operas written to his own texts. (Arrigo Boito, Verdi's best librettist, was a literary-minded composer who wrote his own texts, *Mefistofele* in 1868 and later *Nerone,* but Wagnerian influence cannot be claimed for this, because *Mefistofele* at least was written before the Wagnerian vogue.)

A more successful modification of this Wagnerian emphasis on the poetic quality of the operatic text has been the practice of using recognized dramatic works, abbreviated, but not rewritten, as opera books. Debussy's use of Maeterlinck's *Pelleas and Melisande,* and Alban Berg's adaptations of Büchner's *Wozzeck* and two plays of Wedekind are the most prominent examples. Another method perhaps even more successful has been close collaboration between a composer and poet, each independently celebrated in his own right, as in the case of Paul Claudel and Darius Milhaud; Jean Cocteau and Arthur Honegger; or Hugo von Hofmannsthal and Richard Strauss.

Strauss is the most prominent continuer of the Wagnerian

Gesamtkunstwerk, and it is symptomatic that he has tried various solutions to the problem of the musical drama. In his early un-successful *Guntram* he was poet-dramatist and composer at the same time. But he soon wisely turned elsewhere for his material and scored his first operatic success with a German translation of Oscar Wilde's *Salome.* His famous subsequent collaboration with Hofmannsthal is well documented by their voluminous corre-spondence, which shows clearly the division of labor between the poet on the one hand and the composer on the other. Mutual respect and criticism (with the younger Hofmannsthal usually on the receiving end of the criticism) attest that this was a genuine collaborative effort, and the detailed concern which Strauss evi-denced for the text is impressive. But one is aware that it is the composer speaking and from a musical point of view, as he makes a plea for this or that change, frequently requesting an additional dozen lines or so "in the same mood" for the purposes of a musical effect, with no suggestion of the intricate concern for the minute relationships between words, action and music we have seen so persistently with Wagner. Nor do the works resulting from this collaboration, still less Strauss's later operas, show a greater degree of interrelation among the various elements.

Some of the most *avant garde* experimentation with the musical drama, as for instance that of Alban Berg in his *Wozzeck* and the unfinished *Lulu,* is built upon a basically Wagnerian dramatic structure, with a balance between word and tone which is essen-tially derived from Wagner; but there is no evidence of the detailed correlation which characterizes the Wagnerian synthesis.

Two types of art synthesis where the word is accorded a central position as with Wagner, though entirely independent of the Wag-nerian tradition, are the collaboration of Claudel and Milhaud, particularly in *Christophe Colombe* (especially in the second version of 1952), and the experiments of the contemporary German Carl Orff and his school. Orff, in his production of Shakespeare's *Midsummer Night's Dream,* his *Antigonae* (translation from Soph-ocles by Hölderlin); and above all *Die Bernauerin* (to his own text) has presented the most novel juxtapositions of word, action and music yet produced in the twentieth century. Perhaps the extravagant, grandiose and fantastically unrealizable plans of the theosophical-minded Alexander Scriabin for a *Gesamtkunstwerk* to end all *Gesamtkunstwerke* should be mentioned to complete the record.

Interestingly enough, the creator of the most meticulously Wagnerian art syntheses and the most successful ones since Wagner is not a composer of works for the stage (his only completed opera, the comedy *Der Corregidor,* was not a success), but a composer of lieder. Hugo Wolf applied to his creations in this unique chamber form an attention to minute detail of voice leading, intricate parallel of rhythmic patterns, and in general a consistent respect for the exact emotional connotations of the words, which was consciously in the Wagnerian tradition and most reminiscent of his theory and practice. Wolf's sense of literary values, too, was so far superior to that of any other song composer, or indeed of any opera composer, that it is appropriate to see in him the most direct successor to Wagner, in the matter of a synthesis of poetry and music, at least.

It is customary, and perhaps accurate, to refer to Wagner as the end of an era, and in the sense in which we have been studying him this is indeed true. Bigger and better combinations of the arts are no longer the fashion; the preoccupation with massed effects and the most intense expressivity on the musical stage was a typically nineteenth-century phenomenon (in this respect Strauss and Berg can be considered epigones). Wagner's influence, although it will probably never be completely absent from music and particularly from the lyric stage, is not connected in any vital and dynamic way with his theories of art synthesis nor with his works as examples of it. This fact, however, does not diminish the need to approach his own creations as conscious and very articulate attempts at a *Gesamtkunstwerk,* and a more general understanding of this would result in important new perspectives on one of the most incompletely understood geniuses in the history of art.

Bibliography

Explanation of abbreviations used in the text:

A.S.	Arthur Schopenhauer, *Sämtliche Werke*
E.N.	Ernest Newman, *The Life of Richard Wagner*
H.W.	Johann Gottfried Herder, *Sämtliche Werke*
L.F.L.	*Letters of Franz Liszt*
M.G.	Hans Joachim Moser, *Christoph Willibald Gluck*
M.W.	Richard Wagner, *Briefe und Tagebuchblätter an Mathilde Wesendonck*
R.W.F.	*Richard Wagner an Freunde und Zeitgenossen*
S.G.O.	Ernest Newman, *Stories of the Great Operas*
W.A.R.	Richard Wagner, *Briefe an August Röckel*
W.L.	*Briefwechsel zwischen Wagner und Liszt*
W.M.A.	Ernest Newman, *Wagner as Man and Artist*
W.S.	Richard Wagner, *Sämtliche Schriften und Dichtungen*
W.U.	Richard Wagner, *Briefe an Theodor Uhlig, Wilhelm Fischer, Ferdinand Heine*

Adler, Guido. *Richard Wagner, Vorlesungen gehalten an der Universität zu Wien, 1903–04.* 2nd. ed., Munich, 1923.

Aldrich, Richard. *A Guide to the Ring of the Nibelung.* Boston, 1905.

Bekker, Paul. *Richard Wagner. His Life in his Work.* Trans. M. W. Bozman. New York, 1931.

Berg, Alban. *Lulu.* Klavierauszug mit Gesang. Vienna, [c.1936].

——— *Wozzeck.* Oper in 3 Akten (15 Szenen). Klavierauszug. Vienna, 1930.

Boito, Arrigo. *Mefistofele.* Milan, Naples, Rome, Florence, n.d.

——— *Nerone.* Tragedia in quattro atti. Milan, Naples, Rome, Florence, 1901.

Burghold, Julius. *Der Ring des Nibelungen von R. Wagner.* Text mit den hauptsächlichen Leitmotiven und Notenbeispielen. Mainz, n.d.

Campbell, Thomas Moody. "Nietzsche's *Die Geburt der Tragödie* and Richard Wagner," *Germanic Review*, XVI (1941), 185–200.

——— "Nietzsche—Wagner to January 1872," *PMLA*, LVI (1941), 544–77.

Clark, Robert T., Jr. "Union of the Arts in *Die Braut von Messina*," *PMLA*, LII (1937), 1135–46.

Claudel, Paul and Darius Milhaud. *Christophe Colombe.* Oper in zwei Teilen und 27 Bildern. Klavierauszug mit Text. Vienna, [c. 1930].

Debussy, Claude. *Pelléas et Mélisande*. Drame lyrique en 5 actes et 12 tableaux. Partition pour piano seul. Paris, [c.1907].

Fries, Othmar. *Richard Wagner und die deutsche Romantik*. Zurich, 1952.

Grunsky, Karl. "Klassische Literatur und musikalisches Drama," *Bayreuther Blätter*, XXII (1899), 172–93, 230–65.

Herder, Johann Gottfried. *Sämtliche Werke*. 33 vols., ed. Bernhard Suphan. Berlin, 1877–1913.

Hildebrandt, Kurt. *Wagner und Nietzsche, ihr Kampf gegen das 19. Jahrhundert*. Breslau, 1924.

Hutcheson, Ernest. *A Musical Guide to the Ring of the Nibelung*. New York, 1940.

Indy, Vincent d'. *Fervaal*. Action musicale en trois actes et un prologue. Partition chant et piano. Paris, 1895.

———*L'Etranger*. Action musicale en deux actes. Partition pour chant et piano. Paris, 1902.

Knopf, Kurt. *Die romantische Struktur des Denkens Richard Wagners*. Jena, 1932.

Kobbé, Gustave. *Wagner's Music Dramas Analyzed with the Leading Motives*. New York, 1904.

Koch, Max. *Richard Wagner*. 7 vols. in 3, Berlin, 1907–18.

Kufferath, Maurice. *Guide Thématique et Analyse de Tristan et Iseult*. Paris, 1894.

Kurth, Ernst. *Romantische Harmonik und ihre Krise in Wagners "Tristan."* 2nd. ed., Berlin, 1923.

Lavignac, Albert. *Le Voyage Artistique à Bayreuth*. 4th. ed., Paris, 1900.

Lessing, Gotthold. *Laokoon*. Vols. 9 and 14, erster Teil, *Sämtliche Schriften*. ed. Karl Lachman. 3rd. ed. prepared by Franz Muncker. 23 vols. Stuttgart and Leipzig, 1889–1924.

Liszt, Franz. *Letters of Franz Liszt*. Collected and edited by La Mara. Trans. Constance Bache. New York, 1894.

Mann, Thomas. "Leiden und Grösse Richard Wagners," in *Adel des Geistes*. Stockholm, 1945, pp. 398–471.

Moser, Hans Joachim. *Christoph Willibald Gluck: die Leistung, der Mann, das Vermächtnis*. Stuttgart, 1940.

Neumann, Alfred. "The Evolution of the Concept of the Gesamtkunstwerk in German Romanticism," Unpublished doctoral dissertation, University of Michigan, 1951.

Newman, Ernest. *The Life of Richard Wagner*. 4 vols., New York, 1933–46.

——— *Stories of the Great Operas*. 3 vols. in one, New York, 1929.

——— *Wagner as Man and Artist*. Garden City, New York, 1941, copyright, 1924.

Nietzsche, Friedrich. *Nietzsches Werke*. 20 vols., Leipzig, 1895–1926.

Orff, Carl. *Antigonae*. Ein Trauerspiel des Sophokles. Klavierauszug. Mainz, [c. 1949].

―――― *Die Bernauerin*. Ein bairisches Stück. Klavierauszug. Mainz, [c. 1945].

―――― *Ein Sommernachtstraum*. William Shakespeare. Nach der Übersetzung von A. W. Schlegel eingerichtet und mit Musik versehen. Mainz, [c. 1944].

Patterson, Franklin P. *The Leit-Motives of Der Ring des Nibelungen*. Leipzig, 1896.

Reed, Eugene. "Novalis' *Heinrich von Ofterdingen* as a Gesamtkunstwerk," *Philological Quarterly*, XXXIII (1954), 200–11.

―――― "The Union of the Arts in Brentano's *Godwi*," *Germanic Review*, XXIX (1954), 102–18.

Schelling, Friedrich W. J. *Philosophie der Kunst*. 3. Hauptband, *Schellings Werke*, nach der Originalausgabe in neuer Anordnung herausgegeben von Manfred Schröter. Munich, 1927.

Schopenhauer, Arthur. *Sämtliche Werke*. 6 vols., Reclam, Leipzig, n.d.

Stein, Jack M. "Wagner's Theory of Improvisation and *Die Meistersinger*," *Germanic Review*, XXVII (April, 1952), 96–107.

―――― "Schopenhauer's Influence on Richard Wagner's Concept of the Gesamtkunstwerk," *Germanic Review*, XXII (April, 1947), 92–105.

Strauss, Richard. *Guntram*. In drei Aufzügen. Vocal score. Munich, 1894.

―――― *Salome*. Musik-Drama in einem Aufzuge. Klavierauszug mit Text. Berlin, 1905.

―――― and Hugo von Hofmannsthal. *Briefwechsel*. Gesamtausgabe, Zurich, 1952.

Strobel, Otto. *Richard Wagner. Leben und Schaffen*. Eine Zeittafel. Bayreuth, 1952.

Terry, Edward M. *A Richard Wagner Dictionary*. New York, 1939.

Wagner, Richard. *Beethoven*, in *Sämtliche Schriften und Dichtungen*, IX, 61–126.

―――― *Briefe an August Röckel*. 2nd. ed., Leipzig, 1912. Vol. XI, zweite Folge, *Richard Wagners Briefe in Originalausgaben*.

―――― *Briefwechsel zwischen Wagner und Liszt*. 2 vols., 2nd. ed., Leipzig, 1900.

―――― *The Flying Dutchman (Der fliegende Holländer)*. Vocal score. G. Schirmer, New York, 1897.

―――― *Die Kunst und die Revolution (Art and Revolution)*, in *Sämtliche Schriften und Dichtungen*, III, 8–41.

―――― *Das Kunstwerk der Zukunft (The Art-Work of the Future)*, in *Sämtliche Schriften und Dichtungen*, III, 42–177.

―――― *Lohengrin*. Vocal score. G. Schirmer, New York, n.d.

―――― *The Mastersingers (Die Meistersinger)*. Vocal score. G. Schirmer, New York, n.d.

———— "Eine Mitteilung an meine Freunde," in *Sämtliche Schriften und Dichtungen,* IV, 230–344.

———— *Oper und Drama,* in *Sämtliche Schriften und Dichtungen,* III, 222–320; IV, 1–229.

———— *Parsifal.* Vocal score. B. Schotts Söhne, Mainz, Leipzig, London, Brussels, Paris, n.d.

———— *The Rhinegold (Das Rheingold).* Vocal score. B. Schotts Söhne, Mainz, Leipzig, London, Brussels, Paris, n.d.

———— *Richard Wagner an Freunde und Zeitgenossen.* Leipzig, 1912. Vol. XVII, zweite Folge, *Richard Wagners Briefe in Originalausgaben.*

———— *Richard Wagner an Mathilde Wesendonck. Briefe und Tagebuchblätter, 1853–71.* 40th ed., Leipzig, 1912. Vol. V, erste Folge, *Richard Wagners Briefe in Originalausgaben.*

———— *Richard Wagners Briefe an Theodor Uhlig, Wilhelm Fischer, Ferdinand Heine.* Leipzig, 1912.

———— *Rienzi.* Vocal score. Adolph Fürstner, Berlin, n.d.

———— *Sämtliche Schriften und Dichtungen.* 12 vols., Leipzig, n.d.

———— *Siegfried.* Vocal score. G. Schirmer, New York, n.d.

———— *Tannhäuser.* Vocal score. G. Schirmer, New York, n.d.

———— *Tristan and Isolde.* Vocal score. G. Schirmer, New York, 1906.

———— *Twilight of the Gods (Götterdämmerung).* Vocal score. G. Schirmer, New York, n.d.

———— *Über die Bestimmung der Oper (The Destiny of Opera),* in *Sämtliche Schriften und Dichtungen,* IX, 127–56.

———— *Über Schauspieler und Sänger (Actors and Singers),* in *Sämtliche Schriften und Dichtungen,* IX, 157–230.

———— *The Valkyrie (Die Walküre).* Vocal score. G. Schirmer, New York, n.d.

———— *Zukunftsmusik (Music of the Future),* in *Sämtliche Schriften und Dichtungen,* VII, 87–137.

Wagner, Siegfried. *Der Bärenhäuter.* Vocal score. Munich, 1899.

Walzel, Oscar. *Richard Wagner in seiner Zeit und nach seiner Zeit.* Munich, 1913.

Westernhagen, Curt von. *Richard Wagner, sein Werk, sein Wesen, seine Welt.* Zurich, 1956.

Wolf, Hugo. *Der Corregidor.* Oper in vier Akten. Mannheim, [c. 1896].

Index

Edited by Alexander Brede
Designed by Peter Gilleran
Music autographed by Dr. Carl A. Rosenthal
Set in Linotype Baskerville with Century Schoolbook
and Alternate Gothic type faces